Dress For Transformation

Change Your Clothes, Change Your Life

Shane K Twede

Copyright © 2021 by **Shane K Twede**

All rights reserved. No part of this publication may be reproduced, distributed, or transmitted in any form or by any means, without prior written permission.

Scripture quotations are from The ESV Bible (The Holy Bible, English Standard Version), copyright 2001 by Crossway, a publishing ministry of Good News Publishers. Used by permission. All rights reserved.

Published by Kory Industries
www.koryindustries.com

Request to publish work from this book should be sent to: Shane@Shanektwede.com

Book Layout © 2017 BookDesignTemplates.com
Cover Design by Kory Twede

Dress for Transformation/ Shane K Twede. -- 1st ed.
ISBN 978-0-578-93124-1 Print
ISBN 978-0-578-93125-8 eBook

"Learn to help people with more than just their jobs: help them with their lives."
JIM ROHN

"I will greatly rejoice in the Lord; my soul shall exult in my God, for He has clothed me with the garments of salvation; He has covered me with the robe of righteousness, as a bridegroom decks himself like a priest with a beautiful headdress, and as a bride adorns herself with her jewels."
ISAIAH 61:10

CONTENTS

INTRODUCTION 1
PARADIGM SHIFT 9
UNIFORMS, THEY'RE ALL-AROUND US 11
    Formal Uniforms 11
    Definition of a Uniform 12
    Wearing Uniforms 12
    Observation 14
    Superhero Transformation 16
A BROADER DEFINITION 19
    What is a Uniform? 19
    Expanding the Uniform Paradigm 21
    Uniforms Can be Formal and Informal 24
UNIFORMS' MAGICAL POWERS 27
    External Magic 27
    Internal Magic 33
    The Law of Attraction 34
    The Chicken or the Egg 35
    Affirmations 37
TRANSFORMATIONAL QUALITIES 41
INTERNAL TRANSFORMATION 43
    It's Just Fabric, Right? 43
    Preparation Takes a Little Effort 46

  Free Your Mind 48
  Integrity 50
  Team Dynamics 51
EXTERNAL TRANSFORMATION 59
  Perception is 90% of the Game 59
  What do People Really See? 62
  Chemical Reaction 69
  Team Identity 72
  Uniforms and Teamwork 74
  The Gym Experience 76
  Proficiency 79
THE REAL DRESS FOR SUCCESS 81
  Fake it Until You Make it 81
  Connecting the External with the Internal 84
  Don't Skimp 89
  Passion and Vision 90
  We Are the Embodiment of What We Wear 93
PERSONAL APPLICATION 97
DRESS FOR WHAT YOU WANT TO BECOME . 99
  Goal Setting 99
  Goal Setting Workshop 100
  Uniforms and Goals 113
  Now, What do You Want to Become? 114
  Passions and Occupations Fit for a Uniform 117
  Coloring Outside the Circle 120
SELECTING THE RIGHT UNIFORM 125

- Selection Guidelines 125
- Break the Paradigm. 128
- Selection Criteria Examples 129
- THE CEREMONY, DONNING THE UNIFORM 140
  - The Process of the Under Achievers 140
  - A New Ritual 141
  - Steps for Donning a Uniform 142
- TAKING UNIFORMS TO THE NEXT LEVEL .. 150
  - Uniform Care 150
  - Uniform Cleaning 152
  - Uniform Storage 154
  - Uniform Purchase 155
  - Accessorizing 156
- **TEAM AND BUSINESS APPLICATION** 160
- VOLUNTARY UNIFORMS 161
  - Voluntary Uniforms 162
  - Creating a Voluntary Uniform Culture 164
  - Implementation 165
  - Application 167
- MANDATORY UNIFORMS 170
  - Steps and Considerations 170
  - Share the Reasons 172
  - Requesting Input 173
  - Do They Need to be Identical? 174
- UNIFORM POLICIES 176
  - Components of a Good Uniform Policy 177

    Policy Components 177
    Policy Writing 179
    Policy Communication 179
CONCLUSION 181
    Summary 181
    Next Steps 183
    Final Thoughts 184
Appendix A Goal Setting Steps 187
Appendix B Uniform Selection Guidelines 191
Appendix C The Uniform Ritual 193
Appendix D Resources 195
Other Books By Shane K Twede 201
About Shane K. Twede 203
Acknowledgements 205

INTRODUCTION

Writing a book about clothing, uniforms, and dressing for peak performance is a desire I've had for some time. I'm not quite sure what piqued my interest so profoundly and at such an early age. It may have stemmed from a passionate interest in aviation or a fascination with the military. Seeing soldiers in crisp uniforms can make a lasting impression on a young boy. It might have been seeing people dressed in colorful company uniforms or watching my dad leave for work each morning, dressed in a neatly pressed business suit. Whatever the motivation, I became obsessed.

As a young boy, I had two primary interests, aviation and racing. In aviation, there were men and women who wore sharp looking uniforms and flew all sorts of aircraft. In racing, hydroplanes were my obsession. Many times, my dad took my brothers and me to the lake to watch the races. We saw brave men suit up in colorful uniforms and seat themselves in the cockpits of powerful hydroplanes. I marveled at these amazing larger-than-life characters.

A few of the brave drivers I met back then were Billy Schumacher, Bill Muncey, Dean Chenowith, and

Tommy Tucker Fults. They were not only larger-than-life because of their unique uniforms, they were also incredibly friendly, taking time for pictures or to answer questions from a young impressionable fan.

As a teenager, I followed rock-n-roll bands. Most band members wore unique, if not exotic, looking outfits. At concerts, I pictured myself on stage, wearing these outfits too.

Those early, impressionable days of my youth are long gone, but something about uniforms and their association with proficiency, achievement, and success stuck with me.

At age 13, I got a job as a paperboy. I remember longing to wear the paper sack, a canvas newspaper holder, over my shoulders, like the paperboy who delivered my dad's paper each evening. It had the name of the newspaper boldly stenciled on the front and back: *The Seattle Times*.

Later, I worked at a Shell gas station. On my first day, I was given a generic yellow shirt. A few weeks later, I was handed personalized shirts. My name was embroidered in red over the left pocket. Putting that shirt on gave me a feeling like none I had before—a sense of professionalism—a sense of belonging. I was part of the team now—an official employee of the Shell Oil Company.

Later, I worked my way through college as a cook. Once again, I was given a uniform to wear. As soon as I slipped on the checked pants, white double-breasted chef's coat, and puffy hat, I instantly became a professional cook (at least I looked like one).

It would take some time—even years, before I was actually any good, but the uniform became a prophesy to be fulfilled. It became the shoes I needed to fit into, and there were no shortages of experienced cooks to show me the ropes once they recognized my desire to learn.

It was the same after college when I began a career in aviation. Some of the jobs required formal uniforms, others didn't. Of those that didn't, I'd form my own, at times even sewing them myself. Experienced workers were more willing to mentor me when they could see how serious I was about the job.

As my career matured, and I began leading and mentoring people, I never lost sight of the power inherent in uniforms. By then I had experienced their impact not only on myself, but on others as well.

I had an epiphany while flying airplanes. I started wearing flight suits instead of my usual attire. I remember observing my reflection in the mirror as a competent and professional pilot. In truth, I was an average pilot, but the more I wore the flight suit, and the more I looked in the mirror, the greater my desire grew to become the best pilot possible. If someone saw me in my flight suit, I didn't want them to think I was just some dude trying to look professional. I truly wanted to have the *right stuff*. I wanted the suit to be me, not just me in the suit.

I learned some fascinating…and at times, tough lessons. I found when I wore flight suits, I did a better job planning flights, inspecting the airplanes before flights, and executing flights. I think putting on the suit was enough to bring my awareness to the important task of flying and what it required to be a safe and proficient pilot. In contrast, when I didn't wear flight suits, my flying suffered and my attitude was, for some reason, more casual.

> *Jim Rohn, the great business philosopher, used to say, "Casualness leads to casualty".*

It was this *uniform* epiphany that led me to experiment with uniforms; first on myself, then on sports teams I coached, and ultimately on the teams and organizations I led at various companies where I worked.

In this book, I share the best of what I have gleaned over several decades. I'll explain how people are shaped and molded by uniforms. I'll share how people have fulfilled their dreams, reached greater success, and received more joy and satisfaction after implementing the techniques described in this book. By implementing these ideas, you too can benefit from the transformational powers intrinsic within uniforms.

One more note before we proceed. The transformational powers inherent in uniforms are not exclusive to traditional uniforms. In my experience, almost any wardrobe can become a uniform and generate transformational powers. Even a hat, when used correctly, can bring about amazing results.

Book Outline

The ideas in this book are rooted on observations, experiments, and the proven techniques I've used over the years in both my personal and professional life. I reveal how uniforms have the ability to impact us internally and affect others externally. Detailed information on the utilization and efficacy of uniforms for both recreational and professional teams are included.

I've divided the book into four parts. Below is a brief summary of each one.

Part One:
Paradigm Shift

In this section, formal and informal uniforms and their use are introduced. Information is given on how informal uniforms can be as powerful as formal ones. The section also introduces the internal and external effects of uniform use.

Part Two:
Transformational Qualities

This section details how uniforms, along with other transformational principles, work together to bring about high performance and true success. You will learn that happiness can be achieved today; it doesn't need to wait until tomorrow. In fact, happiness postponed for tomorrow will never bring about true joy.

Part Three:
Personal Application

This is the how-to section. It breaks the transformation process into actionable steps you can take to produce the benefits discussed in Part Two. It also details the most important aspects to adopt if you are serious about high performance and living a pinnacle life. More on this later.

Part Four:
Team and Business Application

In this section, you'll learn how teams, groups, and businesses use uniforms for maximum benefit. Both voluntary and mandatory uniforms are explored along with their implementation and maintenance.

One final thought. Because of your deep desire to expand your knowledge and become all you can, I have a great respect for you. How do I know that's your desire? Because you're reading this book. Not everyone takes their life, the time God gives us on earth, as seriously as you do.

There are many ways to live life well, but only a few leads a person to a pinnacle life; a life that is continually goal-seeking, God-honoring, and people centric. A joyful life is not always the easy life, in fact, an easy life is seldom satisfying, let alone joyful. Give a child everything they want and watch how dissatisfied they become. No, a life well lived is one that takes courage, learning, growth, giving, thankfulness, and love.

The ideas shared in this book are only a piece of the good-life puzzle. By learning these skills and putting them into practice, you will give yourself another step-up in the pursuit of the good life.

Now let's begin this journey together.

PARADIGM SHIFT

Part I

CHAPTER ONE

UNIFORMS, THEY'RE ALL-AROUND US

Formal Uniforms

People in uniforms are all around us. We stop to fuel up and see a gas station attendant wearing a company shirt, often with matching pants. At our favorite coffee establishment, the barista might be wearing a company apron. We may pass by a police or fire station and inside those walls, many will be wearing very identifiable uniforms. To our left, a heating and air-conditioning van passes by, and to the right, a construction truck waits at a stop light. The occupants in both vehicles are wearing company uniforms. Look, there's a school bus heading for the private school two blocks up. All the school kids appear to be wearing uniforms, too.

At lunch, we leave for our favorite restaurant, and on the way there, we see a military convoy with every soldier wearing a uniform. At the restaurant, a cook exits the kitchen to grab a cup of coffee from the wait-station. Yep…even he's wearing a uniform. So, exactly what is a uniform and why do people wear them?

Definition of a Uniform

The word *uniform* can be used as a noun or an adjective. Simply put, in the noun form, it means formal, official, or distinctive clothing worn by members of a team or group. In the adjective form, it means one form, the same form, unchanging or having the same likeness—or is similar.

Let's begin the journey on uniforms employing the definitions above. Then we will greatly expand on them to include, not only formal uniforms, but also informal uniforms. We'll explore how uniforms can greatly affect our day-to-day performance, and how individuals, teams, and groups can obtain far greater success utilizing uniforms.

Wearing Uniforms

Why do people wear uniforms? Well, some wear them because they are compulsory. Others because they satisfy a need, such as offering protection from safety hazards, or enhancing the ability to perform a specific task or function. Others wear them because they like how it makes them feel. There are endless reasons why uniforms are worn. We'll explore a good deal of them over the course of the book.

Like many of you, I have worn various formal and informal uniforms throughout my career/life. At some companies, I was told what not to wear. At others, I was given a formal uniform to wear, and still others, I was given a list or verbally told what my attire needed to consist of on the job.

For most of my career, my uniform consisted of slacks, a buttoned-up shirt, and a tie (and occasionally a suit jacket.) Early on in my management career, if I didn't show up wearing slacks and a tie, I didn't show up—period! Casual Fridays were non-existent back then.

Many years ago, I joined the Civil Air Patrol. It was only for a short period, but in doing so, I had the extreme honor of wearing military uniforms. In the military, uniform regulations are very precise and inspected often to ensure compliance.

Several groups I led had specific regulatory policies and requirements. Uniforms were mandatory for them to ensure their safety as well as state compliance. Some uniforms had special coatings that protected against arc-flash. Those who worked around welding wore even more stringent fire-protective clothing and equipment.

Other groups chose to wear unforms voluntarily for a variety of reasons.

Observation

Throughout the years, as I worked in leadership roles, I noticed how uniforms impacted individual and team performance. Most teams operated at a higher level of productivity and with greater mutual and individual satisfaction and fulfilment when wearing uniforms—but only if certain additional elements were also in place. What were these elements? That is the subject of this book.

For more than 45 years, at both large and small companies, I have sought to get the most out of myself and the teams, groups, and organizations I've led. Every day I endeavored to create higher and higher performance while at the same time, observed what others were doing. Unfortunately, what I witnessed many times were people doing just the opposite. Too many individuals, leaders, and teams seemed satisfied with mediocre performance—just enough to maintain status quo. Why were they okay with performance that barely moved the needle forward? And for some, the needle moved backwards; they were actually becoming more and more irrelevant.

I noticed how their lack of contribution impinged on their self-worth, culminating in even less productivity. It became a downward cycle for them. Many large groups held this low productivity characteristic. Group think is uniform all right, but uniform in an unsettling way, like lemmings. Sure, there were those whose work ethic showed noticeably above the others, but true team synergy for higher performance was lacking much of the time.

Because of these observations, and my own personal curiosity, I decided to make high performance a study. Over the years, I experimented with different techniques. I didn't just experiment at work, I experimented on myself, sport teams I coached, and groups I led outside of business. Many times, I tried these ideas on myself first. If I found success, I tried them on larger groups.

One of the issues I dealt with early on, especially in managerial and leadership positions, was how to offer something as voluntary or mandatory. I remember as a young man (during a brief rebellious period), I wanted to keep my hair long (my idols at that time were mostly rock musicians.) The more my parents, schoolteachers, and church leaders insisted I cut my hair, the greater I dug in and resisted their barrage of pressure tactics. I may have looked hideous with long hair, but cutting it needed to be my idea, the same basic mentality I ran across when making something mandatory. Yes, sometimes I gained compliance, but not enrollment or buy-in. There had to be a better way to get people involved with the decision-making process.

I asked myself, why is it people will wear their favorite sports team jersey without being coerced? What is involved psychologically to cause someone to spend their money to buy a product, then also buy a shirt or hat promoting the very product they just purchased?

Superhero Transformation

Before we continue, I'd like to touch on one other point—and I'll ask it first as a question. Superheroes: what purpose do their uniforms or costumes provide? Do they make the uniform or does the uniform make them? Would they be as effective without a uniform? Does the uniform actually give them power? If so, what power does it give them? When evil individuals see a superhero, are they first intimidated by their outfit? Or is it just the 'POW' and 'WHAM' and clever gadgets.

What happened inside each of these fictitious characters? Most of them had deep-seated issues. Many were extremely shy—even awkward. I'll let this thought percolate for a while inside you. Your mind might be racing to answer these questions, but as soon as you do, chances are new thoughts and questions will likely trickle in.

In the following chapters, we'll explore how important uniforms are for achieving high performance in individuals and teams. We will also examine the impact uniforms have on those around us, and more importantly, the impact they have on ourselves.

Takeaways:
1. Formal uniforms are all around us.

2. Uniform is a noun and an adjective.
3. People wear uniforms for a multitude of reasons.
4. Uniforms and higher productivity go hand-in-hand.
5. Uniforms, along with other elements, create real transformation.
6. We pondered the question—do uniforms make the person or does the person make the uniform?

Chapter 2

A BROADER DEFINITION

What is a Uniform?

Describing uniforms may at first sound like an easy and straightforward task. For example, baseball and football team wear, clothing worn by police officers and firemen, or outfits worn by waiters, waitresses, cooks, and other service-related professionals.

But what is a uniform? Before we go any further, let's break down the definition we used from the previous chapter. The word *uniform* is comprised of a prefix and a word, *uni* and *form*. "*Uni*" means one. A *uni*cycle has only one wheel, a *uni*corn has but one horn. The word *form* is defined as having or giving shape. When someone uses a *form* to create something, the form provides a standard for that shape. A cheesecake is made using a spring*form* pan. The pan creates the shape or form for the delicious cake.

When *uni* and *form* are combined, the definition means one shape; or to put it another way, similar or singular in fashion. That seems to support the examples above, right? Baseball players dress alike—similar fashion. What about police officers? Yep, they dress the same, too, if they are uniformed officers. And that's a good thing. How else would we know if they are the legitimate authority as they walk up to our car window, after we have just exceeded the speed limit?

Uniforms are the outer wear or garments people wear that are similar in nature. All through history, men, women, and children have worn uniforms.

Military outfits were some of the earliest uniforms worn. Those early soldiers wore tunics and protected themselves with armor made from various metals. Later, as technology advanced, soldiers used newer, more advanced materials in addition to camouflage to keep them safe. Specialized equipment was added: helmets, vests, belts, and customized pockets and pouches to carry knives, weapons, ammunition, survival gear, etc. School students were also early adopters of uniforms, as well as religious leaders and those in the medical field.

Careful research goes into many of the uniforms we see today. Huge budgets are spent annually on military and sports uniforms to reduce injury and improve protection. Trends also effect uniforms. The stewardesses of yesteryear dressed much differently than the flight attendants of today. As trends change, so do uniforms.

If you think back into your past or throughout history, are there one or two images of uniform-wearers that come to mind? Depending on your age, different images may emerge. When I think back, I can clearly picture Neil Armstrong in his astronaut suit, taking the very first steps on the moon. For those who are older, it may be Douglas MacArthur, in uniform, onboard the USS *Missouri*. For those who are younger, the image might be of a favorite band member or singer on stage, dressed in special attire. One thing is for sure; uniforms have been with us throughout history, are a part of our lives today, and will be with us in the future.

Expanding the Uniform Paradigm

Here's a thought-provoking question. Do animals wear uniforms? Your initial response might be, "that's an odd question…and I'm not really sure." I'm going to ask you to set aside your current paradigm of uniforms and take a little excursion with me. I promise you; this little excursion or *bunny trail* will be worth your time.

Do chameleons wear uniforms? Do tigers wear uniforms? How about mountain goats? Let's consider these animals and the question I invited you to ponder for a minute. Are tigers' outfits the same as other tigers—singular in form? The definition seems to hold true, but are they really wearing a uniform? A tiger cannot just remove it and change into something else more comfortable. If we add to our original definition of to *have* or to *bear* (not that bear) as a uniform characteristic, that should settle the question. Let's take the infamous chameleon. They are so unique that they can change their uniform, and by changing it, they can look different than the rest of the chameleons—at least until they, too, change colors. So, for some animals, there is individualization.

Why pose this question about animals? The answer? I'm leading you down a carefully arranged path, and if you'll permit me just a bit longer, I'll soon bring this all together, and then we can move to the next point.

Let's take the *uni* in uniform and personalize it, changing the *uni* into your name. For example, if your name is Sally, (input your name) it is now Sally-form. The *form* will represent what you wear—your outer covering. Sally-form translates to the standard clothes, outfits, outer coverings, "uniforms" that she wears.

In Figure 1, the chart has two axes, one in the vertical direction, and one in the horizontal direction. In the preceding paragraph, we discussed how chameleons wear, or possess, similar outer covering with their species. They can also change their coloring depending on the circumstances—usually to camouflage themselves. In a similar fashion, Sally can wear different outfits based on her circumstances, and for every similar situation, she may choose very similar outer coverings or attire as others do.

From the chart below, we see how the chameleon is similar in shape and form to other peer chameleons on the horizontal axis, but in response to environmental situations, it moves up or down the vertical axis changing colors.

Sally is shown on the right side of the chart. Sally is a waitress. Along the horizontal axis we see that she looks very similar in shape and form to her peers—they are all wearing very similar *uniforms*. But Sally is also a mother and a yoga instructor. She also enjoys nights on the town with her husband—she refers to them as *date-nights*. Along the vertical axis, Sally wears very different outfits in response to her environment—like the chameleon. However, for each situation, Sally has complete autonomy in her wardrobe selection—or does she? More on this point later. When she is teaching yoga, her uniform varies little with that of her clients. When she is out on the town, she dresses up, as do most of the people she runs in to at the restaurant she and her husband frequent. When she gets ready for bed, she wears typical pajamas. So, there are standards in form along the horizontal axis and variability along the vertical axis.

24 · SHANE K TWEDE

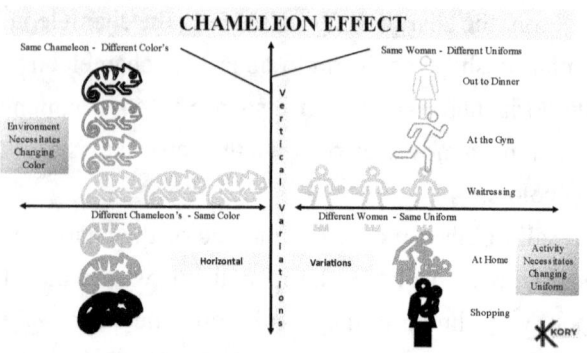

Figure 1: The Chameleon Effect

Uniforms Can be Formal and Informal

Pulling this all together, we have now answered a couple of the questions. What is a uniform? A similar outer covering that may include accessories and equipment. Who wears uniforms? The answer is revealed in the path I just guided you down. I asked you to consider a new paradigm, that every outfit you wear is a uniform, whether it's a traditional and formal one, or an informal and casual one. You see, everything we wear, we put on for a purpose; some serve only a singular purpose while others serve many. If you're going to the gym, you put on gym cloths (most people do, anyway). If you are a white-collar worker, you might wear a business suit or something slightly less casual depending on the office norms. If you are a blue-collar worker, you might have a specific traditional uniform. If not, you probably have clothes that are selected for the best use and durability of the job. If you're a cook, you probably wear a cook's uniform. If you go to church, you might wear a suit or a dress, however, some churches have now yielded to less formal attire. Even if you just throw on some old sweats to wear around the house, those were put on for a purpose—even if it's just to be comfortable or merely to cover up.

The expanded definition of a uniform is this: *All of our outfits are uniforms.* Let me repeat this. All of our outfits...our clothing...and the accessories and equipment we carry on us should be regarded as our uniform. It is important to grasp this concept, as the following chapters will continue to build on this. If you're still struggling with this new definition, hang in there, it will become clearer as we continue unpacking this new paradigm.

Before moving on to the next chapter, let me state an obvious point. If everything we wear is a uniform, it becomes even more important to wear the right uniform for the right situation. But what happens when we don't? How would a casual approach to uniform selection affect us? And how would others perceive us?

There's an all too familiar saying that people shouldn't judge a person based on their appearance. And they would be right, but the truth is, they do, and the failure to realize this is naive. Anyone can wear (to a point) whatever they want. However, to excel in the real world, referred to as reality, one must learn and practice the rules in order to win at this game we call life. Welcome to Reality 101.

Takeaways:
1. We defined uniform as one shape or style; a singular form; similar to others.
2. The Chameleon Effect: Having the ability to alter your appearance and still be similar to others in the same environment.
3. Uniformity and individuality can coexist.
4. A new paradigm: Everything we wear is a uniform.
5. Uniforms can be formal or casual.
6. People do judge us based on our outward appearance.

Chapter 3

UNIFORMS' MAGICAL POWERS

From here on, we'll use the word uniform to represent whatever attire or outfit you wear. Hopefully after the last chapter, you're convinced that everything we wear has a level of consistency as well as a little variability, usually based on the application. Now let's explore the magical powers uniforms possess.

External Magic

The magic of a uniform exists for both the observer and the person wearing the uniform. How many times has someone walked by you or even up to you, and because of their clothing or uniform, you immediately made a judgement concerning them? This judgement may have nothing to do with thoughts of rich or poor, good or bad, or whether you like them or not. It may be just an observation. For instance, your observation may reveal they are a dentist; or that they work outside in the construction business. Maybe it's even a simpler deduction; you notice a patch, badge, or uniform color, and deduce that they work for a particular company.

Now depending on other factors, this judgement may go much deeper. Imagine you're one of three interviewers on a panel for an account manger's position. The dress code for your company is corporate-casual—not suit and tie, but not jeans and T-shirt either. Your first candidate shows up. Her name is Becky. She is wearing a shirt that exposes her midriff and an uncomfortable amount of cleavage.

The next candidate is Carolyn. She is currently the head waitress at a local restaurant. She aspires to a job in the banking industry. She arrives for the interview wearing an inexpensive, but nice pair of slacks and a blouse. Knowing nothing else about the two, who would you hire? Now because of your human resource training, you may hear a voice in the back of your head, screaming, "you can't make that determination!" Can't you? Guess what, you already have…three seconds into the interview. Of course, Becky could have a good story. She might tell you she is a barista. In fact, she may be working three jobs to make ends meet for her and her three children, and that she barely had time between jobs for the interview. All she needs is someone to believe in her and give her a chance. She might apologize that she didn't have anything more professional to wear to the interview, and all her money goes to feeding and clothing her children.

Now how do you feel after your initial impression? My point is not to highlight one's hasty decision process or discuss the legalities of interviewing, but only to give an example of how a person's uniform influences those around them. Remember, in this book we aren't going to kid ourselves, this is Reality 101. Let's try another example.

You're a founding member of a heavy metal rock and roll band. Your group just completed the last performance of its farewell tour (for the 3rd straight year). You finally have a few days off to spend with your 18-year-old daughter. She calls to tell you say she has something special to share with you and your wife, and she'll be over in 15 minutes. When she arrives, she introduces you to the nerdiest dressed teenager you've ever seen. He's wearing ridiculous slacks, a button-up shirt, and a thin tie. Your daughter, on the other hand dresses like you, her dad. She has both her ears gaged up over a half-inch, her hair is a multiplicity of colors and lengths, her face and arms are covered in tattoos, like ones you have…and her clothes are grunge-worthy. She shrieks with excitement, "Dad! I've found the perfect man, and guess what? He asked me to marry him last night!"

How excited are you? At first glance, is he the perfect fit for your daughter? Your family? The thing that is so powerful about someone's uniform is that before they open their mouth or make any gestures, something about them has already made its way deep into the depths of your being. Your mind is at work generating thoughts about this person, just from the magic of their uniform. You might ask: isn't that being prejudice and using stereotypes? Again, this is not a debate on the moralities of your mind. These are examples of how the mind typically works—not all the time, but a fair amount. To deny this because you wish your conscious operated at a higher plane is noble, but probably not very realistic. This is not an indictment on your morality. These are merely observations from living in society; and if the truth be told, we do this very judgement on ourselves—every day. We'll discuss this in more detail shortly.

If uniforms hold "magical powers," capable enough to instantly penetrate your mind, is it possible to direct this power to your advantage? The answer is, of course. That's the whole premise behind the *dress for success* crusade. Here are a couple of examples illustrating just how one could use this to their advantage.

Jerry lives on the street. We aren't sure how he got there, but by the looks of him, he's been there a while: long straggly unkempt hair, wearing the same clothes he's had on for weeks if not months, breath reeking of hunger and stale smoke, and shoes—too small with holes in the toes and heels. As he pushes a shopping cart along the sidewalk, he notices a Help Wanted sign in the window of a small convenience store. Jerry wants off the street. He wants a job. He's tired of being too hot during the day and too cold during the night.

Dress for Transformation · 31

But how? How can he walk in and apply for a job the way he looks? He knows they would never hire him. He looks like a bum, and to make matters worse, he's lost all the self-confidence he once possessed.

Later that day, a man from a local church steps out of a midnight-blue van and hands Jerry a warm meal. Then he reaches into a bag and gives Jerry some clothes, about his size. Jerry thanks the man, and then impulsively proclaims, "I need a job! I know where I want to work, but I can't apply for the job looking like this." The man is instantly seized with compassion. He tells Jerry he'll be back in the morning at the same location to pick him up.

The next morning, sure enough, the midnight-blue van pulls up. Jerry recognizes the familiar face of the kind and compassionate man he met the day before. Jerry hops in the van. Three hours later, the van returns with Jerry wearing new slacks and a dress shirt. His hair is clean and cut and his breath smells of peppermint. Before Jerry steps out of the van, the kind man holds up a mirror and asks Jerry to describe what he sees. Only after Jerry's internal observation of himself becomes congruent with his new external observation does the man tell him he's ready. Jerry thanks him, steps out of the van, and smiles back.

The man calls Jerry back to the van and gives him a card with an address and phone number on it. "Use this address and phone number during your interview," he said. "When you get the job, I will return with the good news." Did Jerry get the job? What do you think?

Here's another example. Kris is a hard worker and has been pursuing a director's position for the company where she works. Three other people in her division are also in line for the position, and they are every bit as capable and experienced as she is. The director in Kris' building, her boss, has a relaxed and casual dress code, but if she were to get the new director's position, she would be transferred to a new location where the dress code for executives isn't nearly as casual.

Kris recently finished a book on how to dress for success. From it she learned when seeking advancement, one should dress in attire resembling those two levels above their current position. She finds this information interesting and recalls it will be leaders two levels above hers that will interview and hire for the new director's position.

She observes what leaders two levels above her are wearing. After visiting a few clothing stores, she begins to wear her "new" two levels up wardrobe (or uniform). Over the next several months, she receives plenty of stares and comments from fellow employees and even her manager about her attire—and not all of them positive. Can you guess who else has observed her new uniform? Yep, other directors and leaders around the company. Every time they see her, they see someone outgrowing her current position.

"Directorship material," they communicate with one another. Guess who got the director's position?

If you're buying a car, and two identical cars are presented to you except one has scratches in the paint and dings in the door, which one are you buying? You see, we all want the best we can get and afford. The right uniform does the same for us. It shows others we are the car without blemishes, we are the car in perfect shape, we are the one who has worked extra hard and is suited for the position. Uniforms not only hold powers to affect others externally, but they also possess even greater powers to change us internally.

Internal Magic

Uniforms have power to change us. Remember Jerry? He was down to his last reserves when it came to confidence. What changed as he stepped out of that van? A haircut, a shower, new clothes? What was it worth? A $10 haircut, a $5 shower, and $70 worth of clothes (which had been donated) for a total of $85. Is that enough to change a person? The answer to this question holds the greatest key to success as it relates to a uniform's magical powers. You see, a uniform not only changes us externally, but it can also change us internally. It works to alter our thoughts which can alter our self-confidence and the value we place on ourselves. You see, Jerry got the job not solely because he cleaned himself up and donned $70 worth of clothes.

He allowed the clothes to transform his thoughts about himself. He walked in and applied for the job, not as a cleaned-up street bum, but as a confident capable applicant, the one he visualized in the mirror before stepping out of the van, and the one who now believes is well suited to help that particular business and their customers.

> *Joe Namath, the football legend, once said, "When you have confidence, you can have a lot of fun. And when you have a lot of fun, you can do amazing things."*

The Law of Attraction

There's a fairly well-known adage that goes like this: If you want to attract something, you must be attractive. We call this simply, the Law of Attraction. It's not enough to want something, you must be ready internally to receive it. Your internal messaging must be congruent with your desires. In dating, some refer to this phenomenon as a person's perfume or cologne. A man desperately wants to date a particular lady only he is continuously rejected by her. Why? Because inside, his internal messaging is negative. It's continuously reinforcing, *I'm not good enough; she's too good for me; I failed in my last relationship, why would she want me? I've never been able to attract a lady like this; I don't have a prestigious job; I don't have a nice car;*

I'm a slob. All this internal talk is his cologne—and ladies can smell it a mile away.

What the lady perceives is his low self-esteem, insecurity, and shallowness. She might also find him rude and overbearing. According to her, he is a turnoff. She's picking up on his internal cologne—which is repulsive to her and will continue repelling her until he changes himself internally. And until he does, his chances of winning her over are likely not going to improve.

Can a uniform modify this fragrance? If so, how? How does wearing a uniform affect the law of attraction? We'll dig into this in the coming chapters, but first let me add a note of clarification. Just wearing a uniform probably won't bring about the magic needed to secure the perfect job or attract a dream man or woman, boy or girl. There's a process one must embrace for the uniform magic to take effect. Just slipping on a business suit won't automatically turn you into a Wall Street baron. There's far more to the process.

The Chicken or the Egg

Our outer affects our inner and our inner affects our outer. Have you ever acted or been in a play of any kind? If so, did you have an opportunity to dress the part or character you were playing? How did it feel?

What about Halloween? Were you ever in a costume or behind a mask and able to really become that character? It's interesting how extreme introverts can become quite gregarious when in character.

Many years ago, my brother and sister, along with a couple of friends, would dress up as a seriously dysfunctional family. My older brother played the role of a long-haired hippy dad; my sister, an old-fashioned mother; and I turned into a nerd with high-water pants, ridiculous wig, and a walk that took weeks to perfect. This was back in the days when nerds were not as well thought of. Two other friends played parts as well, and we all wore worn-out cloths from prior decades.

On the days we transformed into this unusual family, we would select a destination or two to visit. We visited restaurants, theaters, and other unique venues. It was interesting to watch how people reacted to us. We could tell some knew we were just strange teenagers dressed in weird clothes, but others were seriously not sure. No matter what the reaction, we never broke character.

When I think back on those juvenile times, two things come to mind. First, how people treated us. I remember the reaction of those who looked at us as a poor deranged family. My family wasn't rich growing up, but we weren't destitute either. It was the first time I really sensed what some people receive from others, and in that account, it both opened my eyes to a different world, and also made me feel guilty for my role playing.

Second, I was amazed at how in-character I would become, just by adding some old clothes and a wig. I was able to remain in-character even when assaulted by those assuming I was an imposter. I share this embarrassing little story almost in shame, but for this reason: the outer can and will affect our inner just as the inner affects our outer. To wrangle over which one has a greater effect on us or which one comes first is a moot point, they both affect us and are important. It doesn't matter if we are an introvert, extrovert, rich, poor, black, white, schooled, or uneducated. A uniform does indeed have the power to alter our thinking, both for the short term and the long term. Just dressing up and role playing in not enough to make real change. To reap the innate magic within uniforms we need to dig deeper.

Affirmations

Our dominant thoughts are continuously dripping information into our subconscious mind and strengthening what we hold to be true. If subconsciously, we believe we are ugly, changing that internal image of ourselves will be difficult. There have been studies on people who have had plastic surgery to *fix* a self-perceived issue concerning their looks, only to find in many cases that after a successful reconstructive surgery, the patient regards their new looks in the same manor they had before the surgery—even though the issue(s) were made perfect, as attested to by others.

The subconscious mind is powerful, and able to hold the image of being ugly despite their beautiful new look. But there are those who, after surgery, are able to see and accept their new and improved look. How? How can they break through to their subconscious mind? It's by using affirmations.

If you want a change in your life, using affirmations is a good start. It allows new thoughts to drip information into your subconscious mind. Let's take as an example, a person who wants to lower their golf score. If they just think of a new lower handicap, their subconscious mind is usually quick to assert, "yeah right, that's not you"! But through the process of affirmations, they can alter their subconscious mind and actually train and convince themselves that they truly are a low handicapper.

Affirmations synthetically bring a future desire into the present, and the process can yield powerful results. It's playing a make-believe game, only in this game, your subconscious mind listens, learns, and transforms. Once transformed, it is able to affect your conscious mind. If you bring props into the process, it becomes even stronger. A uniform is a prop in aiding the affirmation process. When kids dress up as soldiers, pilots, or princesses, they are touching on this powerful aspect of affirmations.

Tommy wants to be a fireman when he grows up, so what does little Tommy do all day? He dreams of becoming a fireman, dresses up like a fireman, plays with firetrucks, and stops to stare at real fire engines as they drive past.

It's the same with us. If we add theater to our affirmations, they become even more compelling to our subconscious mind. If we want to be a bodybuilder, we dress like one; if we want to have our bosses' position, we dress like them—or their boss; if we want to become a snowboard champion, we buy the name brands and dress and do the things they do.

Is it that simple? It seemed to work for us when we were younger. Of course, as we grew older, and received more information, we may have changed our minds about what we wanted to become. But is it also possible that we changed our minds because we quit dreaming, using affirmations, and dressing the part?

Let's move to the next chapter and see how all this works.

Takeaways:
1. Uniforms affect those around us – Externally.
2. Uniforms have the ability to change us – Internally.
3. The Law of Attraction says we must become attractive in order to attract.
4. The outer affects our inner and the inner affects our outer.

> *5. Uniforms put the affirmation process on steroids.*

TRANSFORMATIONAL QUALITIES

Part II

Chapter 4

INTERNAL TRANSFORMATION

It's Just Fabric, Right?

The most powerful aspect of a uniform is not what others see, but what the wearer sees and perceives. Let's take Ron for example. Ron has an important presentation to give at work. The big boss will be there, and a successful outcome would grant funding for his team's new project. As Ron readies himself at home, he reaches into his closet for a shirt and a pair of slacks, smelling each one to ensure they're clean before he dresses. He steps over to the mirror. It reflects a shirt with a few wrinkles. He feels a hole in the right pocket of his pants. Then he remembers today's presentation will be in the big boss's conference room; ties are mandatory there. He goes back to the closet and reaches for the only matching tie from a broken tie-rack sitting on top of his shelf. As he tightens the tie around his neck, he sees the snag. A memory takes him back to when the snag occurred—last year at his friend's wedding, setting up chairs. When he looks again in the mirror, he's reminded about how much he hates wearing ties. *Ties are for stuffed shirts*; he reminds himself; *I look like my dad*.

He's running late, so off to work he goes. Before his presentation, all he can think about is how nervous he's feeling; and how he wishes he could loosen this noose he's wearing around his neck. His boss points to him, signaling for him to begin the presentation. As he scans the room, he focuses on the big boss. His mind races about, reinforcing his inadequacies as a speaker. *Why did they pick me to pitch this to the big boss? I'm not good at this.* His legs start to shake and his voice cracks. Perspiration wets his armpits. Ron does his best to rise above the intimidation and fears, but inside his inner voice keeps repeating, *you're not worthy; you're not worthy.*

Now let's contrast this to Betty. Betty is in the same situation. She also needs funding for her team's special project, but Betty gets herself ready a different way. She knows formal attire is required for all presentations in her big boss's conference room. So, the night before the presentation she selects an outfit from her clothing that makes her feel important and special. She doesn't need to smell them because she always sees to it her clothes are cleaned and pressed before hanging them up. She takes such great care of her clothes because she spent so much time shopping and thoughtfully considering each article and how they made her feel before purchasing them.

She ceremoniously dresses, with a reminder to herself of how professional she looks in business suits. In fact, she remembers the first time she tried this one on in the store, and how sophisticated she looked and special she felt. Even now, as she observes her reflection in the mirror, the voice inside her declares, "you're special, you're sophisticated, you're one sharp successful businesswoman." As she finishes getting ready, her confidence soars. When she steps up to present, her confidence comes through. She easily works through the charts and information, as she stands tall, and observes the big boss with poise.

I'm not for a minute stating that all you need for success is to wear a unique uniform and to let it transform you. What I'm saying is, along with studying, working hard, and other good habits, don't, and this is the point, forget to also don your uniform. Ron wore clothes, Betty wore a uniform. Therein lies the difference.

When you see your uniform reflection or feel your special clothes against your body, a transformation begins. It's almost as if another person, outside of yourself is confirming the roll you are to play. That person might say to you: you're a professional, you're a role model, you're a great parent, student, businessperson, and you're serious about what you're embarking on.

What is that feeling? It's the feeling of a winner. The feeling of accomplishment and self-confidence that says you care enough about who you are, and what you do, and where you are going. That you take your wardrobe seriously. And in return, your wardrobe responds back by declaring, only a serious person with goals, dreams, and aspirations wears this uniform. You are going places; you will arrive at the destination you are seeking; you are ready!

Preparation Takes a Little Effort

What we see is what we get. If we desire the transformational magic a uniform gives us, we need to put in the time and chose our uniform carefully. Too many times we forget and quickly dress in clothes instead of donning a uniform. What we see truly is what we get. If we've failed to suit up properly, our message back will confirm that. It will communicate to our subconscious and conscience minds all day long, "I'm really not qualified to tackle this task, job, or activity," or "this task isn't important enough to properly prepare for."

We may say, I'm only going to do a quick workout today; changing into the proper exercise clothes is just too much of a hassle—and then later, wonder why our workout was so poor. In aviation, before every flight, pilots are tasked to perform a thorough preflight inspection of the aircraft—and themselves. They must ensure a successful outcome, so expending the effort in advance of every flight is a worthy use of time. Those that don't take this procedure seriously, may deeply regret it. When we don't take the time to don our uniform properly, we only cheat ourselves.

Free Your Mind

Our minds operate similar to the RAM...Random Access Memory in a computer. In other words, just as the RAM in a computer can only hold a specified amount of active data, our conscious minds can only juggle so much at any given time. As our subconscious minds retrieve stored information and bring it into our conscious minds, that also expends gigabits. When you give a presentation from memory, your conscience and subconscious mind are communicating back and forth. The subconscious mind is a bit of a maverick and will many times deliver to the conscious mind information that wasn't asked for.

Let's continue with our presentation example. What would happen, if along with receiving information about Slide 8, our subconscious mind sends up a message saying we look ridiculous? Then we feel the car keys tickling our leg through a hole in the pants pocket and are reminded that we still haven't taken our slacks in to be mended. Our inner voice screams, "Your pants are worn-out, just like this presentation." We look into the eyes of those seated around the conference room table and make a hasty judgement. "They're more professional than I am." Then we lose our confidence, and the presentation deteriorates.

But what if along with the information about Slide 8, the message from our subconscious mind says; "You've got this; you're looking good. This will be your conference room table soon enough." Which internal conversation leads to a more focused and powerful presentation? One conversation leads to more destructive self-talk and circular internal dialogue. This type of internal dialogue tends to clutter your RAM. When your RAM becomes cluttered with self-deprecating thoughts, the space you need to successfully retrieve information is compromised.

We sometimes hear people say during a presentation, "I'm sorry, I forgot where I was going with that point," or "Where was I now?" I once had a college professor who would ramble at 90 miles-per-hour while scribbling (mostly illegibly) on a chalkboard. Then he would stop, turn to the class, tap his head, and say, "computer slipped." In his case, maybe his subconscious mind wasn't retrieving the information as fast as his hand could write. Although a more likely explanation is that he overloaded his Random-Access Memory or mind.

Confidence and self-esteem help free our minds for attracting the things we truly seek. A clearer mind helps us focus on the subject at hand, whether it's a presentation at work, or getting to know that special someone when out on a date. Careful selection of a uniform and proper preparation will help remove the negative and circular chatter our subconscious mind tries to impose upon us during the most inopportune times. A positive clear conscience grants us the freedom and RAM space needed to be us—at our best. Negative subconscious thoughts often intensify, creating an aggravation of circular patterns. Many of these thoughts stem from feelings of inadequacy. By adopting a uniform process, our conscious and subconscious minds can be bolstered up, and not just temporarily.

Integrity

When our inner and outer selves are congruent, a whole new world opens up for us. People are more willing to go along with our views, and they are more willing to buy from us when we're selling. We actually become more attractive in the eyes of those around us. They smell a different fragrance, one of sincerity. Trust and confidence are almost instantaneously achieved. How is that possible?

When someone says, "That person's a little shady," they're really saying, "I don't trust that person." They're thinking something isn't lining up in what that person is saying, doing, or how they're behaving. It might be very subtle, but when a person has internal/external duplicity, others notice. It may take some time, but eventually a person's integrity shows through. It will either hang on them like a cheap garment or fit them like a luxuriously tailored suit.

A person without integrity wears a costume—and they act; a person with integrity wears a uniform—and they're authentic.

Team Dynamics

Most humans have an innate sense of belonging. We are, after all, social beings. And what better way to show that sense of belonging then to outwardly model that for others. We discussed briefly how people wear shirts brandishing their favorite sports teams, especially when their teams are doing well or have just won a championship. Why is that?

The external aspect we'll cover in the next chapter; the internal aspect we'll unpack here. I'm a football fan. Even though my favorite team is not from Seattle, where I live, I'm more familiar with the fan base here. The fans refer to themselves as the 12th man (only eleven actually play on the field). Football jerseys, hats, and coats can be seen everywhere, in restaurants, hardware stores, gas stations, and yes, football stadiums.

By wearing a piece of uniform, an individual quickly aligns themselves with their favorite team. So much so, that when their team loses, some fans are seriously depressed the rest of the day, if not the entire week. They have so identified with their team, that inside themselves, in some illogical way, believe they are actually part of the team. Applying face make-up and color to their hair takes this to an even greater level. For many, identifying with a team gives them a sense of belonging. It makes them an active participant in the winning—and losing.

After a successful game, the fans don't scream, "They won!" They scream, "We won! We won!" They became what they wore. Now this particular phenomenon can take place without wearing a uniform, but wearing a uniform most certainly fortifies this connection.

In one organization I managed, we implemented a high-performance team structure. Every team whose uniforms were not mandatory by regulation had the option of wearing uniforms. Some chose to only wear matching shirts, some pants and shirts, and others chose not to wear uniforms at all (of course, they still wore clothes). Those who adopted uniforms in their groups exhibited several unique and positive attributes. The external attributes again will be discussed in the next chapter, but the internal attributes and characteristics were honestly the most impressive.

Some of the team members who previously were somewhat antagonistic to the greater direction of the organization and in particular, their teams' mission, were suddenly onboard. And not only were they onboard, but many became leaders for change, innovation, and productivity. The results were astonishing. When I visited these teams, no longer did I see wall-flower employees, but excited leaders desperately wanting to show me what they were working on. Issues between team members didn't magically disappear overnight, but in many cases improved to become almost nonexistent.

I was thrilled to watch these men and woman step into their greatness. Whatever held them back previously was gone. When they fully aligned with their team, suddenly, they had the autonomy to make the changes necessary to succeed. And their success was not just realized at a company level. The biggest success and rewards were to them personally.

There are other actions necessary to implement a high-performance organization than just offering uniforms, but this one action can be a significant one. As groups voluntarily adopt uniforms, they assert they belong together. Each person embraces a belonging to the other team members and desires to be identified with them visually. Once a person identifies with a team, group, person, company, etc., they now have skin in the game. The team's purpose is no longer something vague and distant, but recognizable and intimate. There's a promulgated mantra heard lately in management: *hearts and minds*. Every leader I know would kill (a figure of speech) to have their team's hearts and minds pulling in one direction for the betterment of their company. Uniforms can help in this.

Uniforms also declare, "I am a professional." Those in the military probably know this best. Once a person strolls through a corridor wearing Navy whites, or Air Force blues, they join the ranks of all the soldiers that have gone on before them. Not long ago, every soldier walking through an airport was applauded. They were applauded for defending their country—yes; but also, for the discipline and the sacrifice it took to endure the long and intensely harsh training. People see the uniform and know instinctively; they are professional and disciplined. They can do the job, they are worthy.

When a soldier dresses, and with each piece of uniform that was so carefully cleaned, pressed, and polished, their mind confirms they are worthy to wear it. They might assert, "I belong; I am a fellow brother or sister in the Marines, Army, Navy, Coast Guard, Air Force, or Space Force."

Most uniforms have an affirming affect. Wearing a military, fire, or police uniform may signal to the wearer the price they paid to earn that right. That heavy price sinks into their subconscious. That person made it through boot camp, or passed physically exhaustive drills and tests, or practiced until they possessed true marksmanship.

A gym uniform can also feed the subconscious mind and bolster your inner drive. Try this experiment. Next time you go to the gym, slip on whatever you find available. Don't think about it, just put on clothes, and head to the gym and do your exercise. Then compare that workout to one where you carefully selected your gym clothes. They may be ratty looking, that doesn't matter. What does matter is how your clothes make you feel. Make sure you add a little ceremony to the "getting dressed" process (more on this later). Once you get to the gym, stop in front of the mirrors (preferably in the locker room so you don't embarrass yourself). Add a hat and headphones, (if so inclined), and slip on your gloves (if you use them).

Now with each added accessory, breathe in strength. See yourself as the man or woman dressed for a serious and successful workout. As you tighten your shoes laces, focus on why you are wearing these shoes; think about their design and function. Do you remember buying them? Now enter the gym like a gladiator would enter an arena for competition. Breathe in deep and confirm within yourself that you are well-suited to win—win over any and all weaknesses that may have been there earlier. Weakness from pain, a bad day at work, feelings of mediocrity, or fatigue. Now speak these words. "I'm ready, ready for this workout and my moment of greatness."

Which workout do you think will turn out better? I think you can guess. Earl Nightingale revealed this thought many years ago. He said, "You become what you think about." Many years before that the Bible revealed, "As a man thinketh in his heart, so he is." A uniform is a device and an aid that allows you to align your thoughts with your desires. If you want to go to the gym and punish your body so it can change and grow—dress the part. Let your uniform reveal in the conscious mind how serious you are. Then your conscious and subconscious will go after what you desire.

Takeaways:
1. The most valuable aspect of a uniform is not what others see but what the wearer sees and perceives.
2. Preparation takes effort, but the rewards are great if we put in the time.
3. Free the mind's RAM of negative self-talk by not dripping negative visual images into the subconscious mind.
4. Maintain integrity. Always ensure the inner and outer are in sync.
5. The need for affiliation and belonging is strong. High-performance team members desire to self-identify with their teammates and team purpose.

Chapter 5

EXTERNAL TRANSFORMATION

Perception is 90% of the Game

Uniforms change our external appearance, which has an effect on those around us. Regardless of the uniform we wear, be it a properly selected and well purposed one or an unintentional meaningless one, our uniforms affect us internally, as described in the last chapter. Similarly, what we wear has an effect on others, positive or negative. Part of the effect occurs when our attire influences our inner self-awareness and is then portrayed outwardly for others to see.

Another element is less complicated. Let's call it human nature. People tend to make instant judgements based on looks. However, when we select a uniform that aligns with our goals and desires, and then add a little fanfare (called the uniform ceremony), we can change how we feel internally and ultimately how we act externally. This process influences those around us.

People step aside when someone dressed in authority walks past. Why is that? Before answering, let's first discuss perception. We spend a great deal of our lives perceiving things around us. Is it safe? Are these people friendly? Can this person help me? Is she kind? Does he like me? Does this doctor really know what's wrong with me? Is it going to rain? Is the weather broadcaster correct? And on and on and on it goes.

Let's take an example of a stranger asking for our name. Our mind immediately goes to work trying to determine who this person is and what their motives are. In fact, our mind probably began the perception process even as the person walked towards us. When a person wears a uniform, we employ their image in our perception process. If a fireman walks by, we think…there goes a fireman. If we see a lady in a yoga outfit…there goes someone who's into their health, and so it goes. If we see a person in rags sleeping next to a shopping cart full of the same, we think…this person is homeless.

In life, called reality, we use first impressions to make first judgements about a person. Whether we intend to judge people is not relevant. Our mind is a judging factory. We make judgement calls throughout the day—every day. "Should I eat this? Should I fill up with gas here? Should I place the call to my in-laws today or wait until tomorrow? Should I ask for a raise? Should I turn here?" Life places us in situations, all day long, where we must use the judging faculty in our brain.

This is why first impressions are so important. People judge us by what they see. Now, of course, once they get to know us and acquire more information, they can make a better determination about us, but at first, it's all about perception. It's alleged that when a job candidate enters the interview room, interviewers have already made up their mind about hiring that candidate in the first few seconds—many times before the candidate has opened their mouth.

Your outer shell, your uniform, is important in influencing those around you. Some people don't care how they look or how they present themselves. Many aren't concerned about impressing others, and that's perfectly okay—there's no judgement here; however, this book is written for those desiring a pinnacle life that places themselves on the road to personal and professional success and happiness.

What do People Really See?

When people observe your uniform, what do they really see? First, they see what the uniform represents. If it's a professional trade uniform, they might think—there's an air conditioning specialist, or there's a waiter. If a person is wearing an expensive suit, the observer might conclude they are a high-powered businessman or businesswoman. If the uniform is sloppy and unkempt, the observation may be that the person doesn't care how they look, or that they don't have the money to buy nice clothes or that they don't care to keep them properly cleaned and pressed.

Thoughts like these are first impressions and may only last for a split second before another observation takes over, the second impression. In the second impression, additional visual cues are added to make an assessment. The mind might observe accessories or equipment. One might now see that a man has a patch on his uniform with the name of the company or that a guard has a holster with a gun. A second impression might pick up on a nice set of earrings, or a brand-name purse.

The main cues picked up during the second impression gives the uniform wearer context. Take, for example, a person wearing a uniform of baggy pants, hoody sweatshirt, gold chains and new basketball shoes with two burly men standing on either side of him, and people running up to ask for autographs. Your second impression reveals that this person might be a famous basketball player or an artist—maybe a rapper.

There's a third impression, regarding who is inside the uniform. This impression is even more fascinating. It's about how we can perceive a person's temperament in a very short period of time. We sometimes hear people say, "I knew the minute I saw them we would get along." This impression I call the transparency effect. An example of this is when a person feels happy and positive. As they walk through a store, observers smile at them for no apparent reason. Some even say hi to this perfect stranger. Observers sense this person's attitude and character beneath the uniform.

To recap, the first impression is about your outer uniform—your clothes. The second impression is about your accessories, condition of your uniform, physical appearance, and other additional visual cues. The third impression is the transparency effect. It's the ability to sense your disposition, attitude, and belief about yourself. We observe people, create impressions, and fashion a quick judgement on those perceptions—all in just a few seconds.

When a person's not feeling special, maybe because they didn't take the time to make their uniform a priority, it reflects on their inner self, as we discussed in the last chapter. This person could walk all the way through a store or across the office and not get one smile or hello. All because the uniform and their inner self are not radiating success, happiness, and contentment.

Some people bristle at wearing professional uniforms. Take for instance, Cindy, who works in a dentist office. Cindy is required to wear a uniform, but she finds it very unattractive. She and several others at the office, have asked for new uniforms, but their appeals have been largely disregarded. Because Cindy feels unattractive in her uniform, she makes it a point never to wear her uniform to the store. So, every night after work, she goes straight home. One night she works much later than usual. She had put off grocery shopping that week, and now, she and her cat are out of food. She decides, reluctantly, to stop at the store on her way home. Once inside, she hurries through the aisles as quickly as she can, hoping she is not seen or recognized.

When other shoppers notice Cindy, what do you think they see? Do they see a person who is proud of who they are and where they work? Do they see a professional? Possibly, but only for a split second before seeing what is behind the uniform; an embarrassed person who isn't radiating professionalism. Would onlookers think to themselves, wow, that would be great to work where she does. Probably not.

But what if Cindy became one with her uniform. Instead of letting it sour her self-confidence, she embraced it. She might acknowledge it's not the trendiest uniform, and sure, the boss should spring for a wardrobe upgrade, but regardless, she's proud of where she works and what she does. The uniform, even with its deficiencies could confirm in her the professional she is.

Now as she strolls through the supermarket, what do people see? It's a completely different experience. Children might stare at Cindy and think to themselves, someday I hope to wear an outfit like that and walk through the store. I bet she's important.

Men and women make, or break, business deals all day long based only on first and second impressions. Negotiations, whether for a job interview, purchasing items like cars, or even communicating with children are influenced by impressions. Even discussions with friends, coworkers, bosses, and neighbors are affected by impressions.

The ability for others to like us in many cases begins with a first and second impression. Many people won't get an opportunity for a third impression. A lady looks out the window and recognizes her neighbor who lives up the street. She also notices his dog in her yard without a leash—and she's not happy. After all, she just had new bark raked in last month. She sees the dog's owner walking casually toward the dog. Almost immediately, she makes a judgement call concerning her neighbor, and it's not good. She turns from the window in disgust. What she failed to see because of her brief visual encounter was that his dog had broken free of its leash and ran into her yard. She also didn't see her neighbor cleaning up the mess. She didn't see any of that because she turned away after her first impression. If they run into each other in the store or in the neighborhood, how amiable will this lady be towards him? All because of first impressions.

Once a person is seen sloppily dressed, it will take numerous new observations and additional information to offset that first impression. If we only have one encounter, that first impression will become our identity for that observer maybe forever. Their interpretation of us is not ours, but theirs—correct or incorrect.

There's another story told that goes something like this. There was a man seated at a train terminal with his five children. An observer, sitting close by, watched his five children running up and down the hall, screaming and creating a disturbance. They knocked over a display, spreading pamphlets across the floor. The observer, trying to read, became more irritated by the second. She glared at the children and could see they were not disciplined or well cared for. They were dirty and wearing outfits that didn't match. Finally, the lady had enough, and marched over to the father to give him a piece of her mind. After all, she thought, if someone wants five children, they need to learn how to control them. Oh, she was indignant.

Those were her first and second impressions.

Here's how the father responded to her verbal lashing. "I'm terribly sorry for their behavior. I guess I…I hadn't noticed. You see, their mother died yesterday…and I'm waiting for my sister. She's coming in from Chicago to stay with them until I can figure out what to do. There's no one to leave them with, so I brought them here with me. They're really good kids. I love them so much, and they're usually quite well behaved. I'm sure they're just confused and upset right now. Children? Children? Come sit over here with me, please."

That's a tough story, isn't it? First and second impressions can be wrong so many times. Even so, impressions are real, and people do make judgement calls on them—right or wrong.

Knowing this enlightens us, and we can use this information for our benefit; after all, striving to make the most of someone's first and second impression of us is desirable. They won't always get it right. We can't control what other's think, but we can influence them greatly by improving how they see us.

Chemical Reaction

Earlier we discussed the invisible perfume or cologne one possesses. This can either work for or against us—attraction or repulsion. Let's dig a little deeper into why this occurs. There's a theory called modeling. Simply stated, if you model a certain behavior and another person has a similar behavior, that person is more likely to relate to you. You will in fact have an affinity towards each other. If John wears sports jerseys and drinks beer, and Fred wears sports jerseys and drinks beer, it won't take much for these two to connect at a surface level.

Now this doesn't work every time, but you get the idea. If John shows up to work always wearing a suit and tie, and those around him don't, he will be the puzzle piece that doesn't fit in. Those around him may have a difficult time receiving him into their inner circle. If Joanne, who dresses in business suits joins the team, it is likely that she and John will possess an immediate affinity toward each other, strictly based on their attire or uniform.

Several years ago, a president and a vice president at one of the large companies where I worked had differing views on attire. When it wasn't necessary (for business reasons) to wear a formal suit, the president dressed more casually. The vice president, on the other hand, was never seen without a suit and tie, regardless of the business setting. One was trying to change the culture with his relaxed uniform while the other stuck to the company's more traditional uniform. During a company meeting, where both men were present, the dichotomy between them became very apparent. In fact, a debate regarding each other's attire broke out on stage for all the audience to witness. Each leader tried convincing the other (and an audience of managers) how their attire related to the culture they desired, almost to the point of insulting each other. Neither gave in to the other one's viewpoint. It was quite a cringeworthy spectacle.

In the end, neither man was wrong, each just felt more comfortable wearing different style uniforms. Each of them felt their style brought about the desired culture they were looking for. By the way, these two never became close working partners as far as I could surmise, and soon they both left the division. One moved to a different part of the company, and one left for an executive job at another company.

Attraction and rejection go far deeper than just what the eyes behold. When you connect with another, dopamine, the feel-good drug is released. Have you ever noticed, and I'll refer to single people for the sake of correctness, that when seeing someone you think is attractive, a feeling comes over you—a good feeling, like you want to get to know them. What about the opposite? You see someone that is unappealing, maybe due to their clothes or something you just saw them do, or a feature in them that for some reason reminds you of someone you dislike. Any dopamine hit? Nope—nothing. Can this change? Of course.

What if this person turns around, takes off their glasses and exposes astonishing sapphire eyes—the kind that draws you in. Maybe now you're sensing a little dopamine hit. What if you see a patch on their coat, displaying your favorite band? Is the hit of dopamine getting stronger? Now this person, after a quick discussion with you, rolls up their sleeve to expose a tattoo—the same tattoo you have on your arm. Okay, hopefully you see the point. Let's move on.

Team Identity

Earlier we touched on team dynamics and how uniforms help fulfill a need in each of us for belonging. Uniforms give us the means of identifying ourselves with others of our choosing. Now we'll look at how uniforms help in team identity.

Let's begin with sports uniforms. Having teams wear matching outfits is highly desirable. Why? Can you imagine a football game where all the players are dressed differently? How difficult would it be for the quarterback to quickly scan the field and find an open receiver? There would probably be a lot of interceptions. During the kickoff return, who do you block? Everyone looks different, and yet the same. I think you would agree it would be very difficult for a team to be effective. Those who have played street football with sizeable teams know all too well this challenge.

What about the military? What if (and this occurs), warring sides can't easily distinguish between friend or foe? You've no doubt heard the term friendly fire. Well, that becomes much more prolific when uniforms are not used. In WWII, the United States lost too many soldiers due to misidentification, and that was with uniforms. Deaths during combat would be magnitudes greater if uniforms were not utilized. Uniforms serve a life and death purpose during war.

What about a more regular job? If a trade person shows up at your door to fix your broken refrigerator in jeans and a T-shirt, would you question their company affiliation? You might also question their technical expertise as well. A uniform helps to solidify their affinity to all that their company stands for—good and bad.

Let's say you work late and decide to stop off at your local fast-food joint for a quick (and unhealthy) meal. The woman behind the counter is wearing sweats. You notice the rest of the employees are all wearing uniforms. The woman asks you for your money. How eager are you to hand it over? Why? Because in your mind you have a conflict. You're wondering if this woman actually works there. She may, but your mind is working automatically on perception. Now if she shares that the duty manger left because his wife is at the hospital having a baby, and she is the assistant manager and was abruptly called in to help, that will probably settle your anxiety. With this new information you're able to see past your initial perception.

Uniforms and Teamwork

We will introduce the topic of uniforms and teamwork here, then later on we will examine this topic in greater detail.

There are numerous methods for building teamwork and high performance. Wearing a uniform is only a part of the teamwork tapestry. Can a team be high performing without the clear use of uniforms? Maybe, but what I've observed over the years is that uniforms play a role in most high-performing teams in some fashion or another. As we covered earlier, high-performing teams, when given the option, may organically adopt a uniform policy. Why? Because they seek positive affiliation. They're proud of the work their team accomplishes. They respect each team member and want to show off their exclusivity with others. When others see their uniforms, it makes them feel good—special. They know that the person is seeing a top-notch member from an elite group—whatever that group happens to be.

Some teams don't buy into matching shirts or full uniforms. Sometimes it's just a hat, a patch, or something else relatively simple. Some teams choose to reject all forms of uniforms, preserving their individuality. Interestingly however, many times the teams who reject coordinated uniforms end up dressing virtually the same anyway. This can happen whether it is a high-performing team or not. It stems from the affinity and need for belonging. Even people and teams that are adamant about clothing freedom end up dressing similarly.

There are also those who try going counterculture. Remember those who first wore baggy pants down to their knees? Soon they were met with clones who did likewise. I remember a group of leaders who, although they didn't like each other much, had to work together. In a short period of time, they began dressing nearly identical. One of them, who had just been recently elevated as their boss, wore unappealing sweater vests. Within months, all those in his leadership team were wearing these ghastly faux-pas fashion statements. (Sorry, my taste is inserted here). Sometimes it's the bootlicking syndrome when a group dresses like their boss. Sometimes it's a craving for affinity and belonging. Either way, it's interesting how this dynamic plays out time and again—even unknowingly with staunch opposers of anything uniform related.

Let's now return to how uniforms influence us externally and leave the more in-depth discussion on teams for later. A uniform proclaims professionalism, or one who belongs to an organization or affiliation. A person wearing a uniform may also take on merits of that uniform. For instance, a person wearing a shirt displaying their favorite baseball team logo also demonstrates their affinity to that team. As an onlooker, we identify that person as a fan of "such-n-such" team. We see another person wearing a rock band tour T-shirt. We might conclude that person went to the concert and bought the T-shirt, therefore they must like the band. If we also like the band, we might give the person a thumbs up. We might even engage with them in a short conversation. "Yeah, I wanted to go to the concert, too, but couldn't get the time off." We have aligned with them strictly based on our mutual adoration of a band discovered simply by viewing their shirt *(or uniform)*.

The Gym Experience

One day at the gym, I decided to make an informal study of the members' various exercise apparel (and still managed to get a workout in). The majority of the men and woman in the free-weight area were all wearing similar type uniforms. Most had on shorts or sweatpants, and a tank-top, sweatshirt, or equivalent. None of the clothing looked particularly expensive or fancy. A powerlifter showed up wearing something very different. In an instant, all who were there could see this person was not your run-of-the-mill iron clangor. His lifting suit, not yet pulled up, hung around his waist. He set his bag down with a loud clank, then pulled out chains and other serious gear. Within minutes, teenagers circled him, asking him questions. "Who are you? Are you a professional powerlifter? How much can you bench?" As he worked out, many stood and watched. Prior to his arrival, the free-weight area had been in more-or-less uniform equilibrium. Now with the addition of a professional powerlifter, all that changed.

In another part of the gym, where complex machines of steel, cables, and weights stretched out over several rows, a man wearing jeans, boots, and a bulky shirt was hard at it. Instead of wearing the latest leather or high-tech exercise gloves, he had on a pair of cheap blue non-skid rubber gloves, most likely purchased from his local hardware store. As he clunked away at the gym equipment, he received stares, too—especially when he had difficulty understanding how to make a few of the machines operate. Most of those who stared, made it brief and moved on—some giving a smirk to their workout partners as they passed.

Upstairs on the treadmills, men and women wore expensive looking gym outfits—many from the same company. How did I know? They proudly exhibited logos on their attire for all to see. In the studio rooms, there were mostly ladies dressed in form-fitting yoga pants and shirts—again displaying similar company logos. I watched the scene at the gym as one curiously watches animals at a zoo. Yes, I should have been focusing on my workout, but for a few interesting minutes, I stopped to marvel at the gym dynamics.

When we were young, many of us learned the story about the ugly duckling. How this poor ugly duck was not like the others. The prettier ducks took offense just because he was different, and later learned he wasn't a duck at all, but a beautiful swan.

Now in the children's story there was a moral to the story—don't judge a book by its cover; but as I observed the gym dynamics…people do, for good or bad. I share the gym observation not for another lesson on morality, but additional examples on reality and how the world works. If one is seeking success in this world, they need to first understand *reality*. Affinity and belonging are powerful needs each of us have (the gym example reinforces this). Yes, turning the world upside down and sideways is a noble goal. The world certainly needs people who will color outside the lines and push the boundaries; but keep in mind the power of uniform. Modeling group uniform will place you in the inner circle faster. If you want to change the world, the best place to start is to understand it first.

Proficiency

Model experts in the field you desire proficiency in and mimic every nuance of that expert to fast-track learning.

Purchase a pass to the inner circle by observing and wearing an appropriate uniform. By wearing a uniform similar to your mentor's, you can position yourself for success. Once there, you can move the group or team to a higher level if desired after first becoming an insider. Employing a uniform is an effective method to help break through the bureaucracy of mistrust.

Study those in your field of expertise. As your boss dresses—so should you. As your fitness star dresses—so should you. Test out this approach and see if it doesn't increase proficiency.

If one wants to be the best *team player*, dress as a team player. If the team tucks it in, you should tuck it in. Afterwards, when the team dynamics are good and you have secured your place as an elite contributor, then you can suggest that everyone untuck, but for now, let the uniform do its magic.

> ***Takeaways:***
> *1. People are judging machines, for good and bad.*
> *2. People are able to perceive more than the uniform; they can perceive what's behind the uniform.*
> *3. Modeling can bring about a chemical reaction.*
> *4. Uniforms offer identification and belonging.*
> *5. Uniforms often lead to greater teamwork and performance.*
> *6. The affinity effect is strong; it draws at us all.*
> *7. One can quickly become proficient by modeling others and then can rise from the affinity plateau if desired.*

Chapter 6

THE REAL DRESS FOR SUCCESS

In contemplating the familiar adage, *dress for success*, you should first determine what success is. And more importantly, what success is for you. If uniforms help facilitate what we want to become, then…what do we want to become?

Fake it Until You Make it

How many times have you heard this phrase or something similar: "fake it until you make it?" Although this phrase might resemble an affirmation, it isn't, and neither is just dressing for success. Neither is what this book is about. You see, faking it just makes one a fake. A movie aired in 1967 entitled "*How to Succeed in Business Without Really Trying*". I rather enjoyed the movie for its comedic value, but for a course on how to succeed, I found it frightful, at least for most of the storyline.

To summarize, and I'll leave the moral of the storyline out since it's overtly obvious, the character, J. Pierpont Finch was a window washer. After reading a book titled, "*How to Succeed in Business Without Really Trying,*" he obtains a job in the mail room of a big company. Using the plan described in the book, he quickly ascends the company ladder. How did he do this? By faking his way, dressing for success, and misleading his bosses into thinking he was a hard worker.

He stole other's ideas, hoodwinked his bosses into thinking he attended the same college they did, and many other deceitful schemes. In one scene, J. Pierpont Finch arrives at work just before his boss. He messes up his desk and his clothes, then lays his head down. When the boss comes in, he sees J. Pierpont Finch, the young worker, sleeping at his desk and thinks to himself, *he must have worked through the night.* The boss commends him for his dedication to the company. Dedication? Hardly. He was a full-time faker.

I don't believe in the fake it until you make it mindset. I'm not saying it can't occasionally bring results, but success? Hardly. For an affirmation to work, for *dressing for success* to work, one needs to desire the outcome and believe fervently in that transformation. If one reads an affirmation but does not align with that affirmation and *put in the work* of transformation, then those words remain just that—words. They will never have the power to make the internal transformation that truly bring external changes.

Faking something is disingenuous. It means you want something for nothing without having to work for it. Dressing in a uniform without aligning yourself to it makes it just a costume. For a uniform to hold its magical powers you cannot fake it. I'm sure we have all heard stories of crooks dressed in police uniforms, fooling unsuspecting citizens. The uniform no more makes the crooks cops than chameleons becoming trees. However, if a boy or girl, desiring greatly to become a police officer when they're older, wears a police costume, that costume can actually change that child's belief and ultimate trajectory. It can become a powerful self-fulfilling prophesy.

Dressing for success is not about faking it 'til you make it. It's about seeing yourself honestly in the present, while concentrating on what to become in the future. A true uniform creates tension between the present and future. Better stated, you see your goal so clearly in your mind's eye, that you believe it to be true in your heart. If it is true in your heart, then to realign yourself, you must dress appropriately. To not dress for success would be to outfit an outdated image of who you are.

Jesus said in Mark 11, "Whatever you ask in prayer, believe that you have received it, and it will be yours." Jesus is asking us to be one with our petitions to him. Not ask and wish it but ask and know it—that's real belief. In the same way, when you wear a uniform that represents what you want to become or who you are, make sure your belief is strong, and you're aligned from the inside out and outside in.

Connecting the External with the Internal

When you desire a goal or future strong enough, it's possible to obtain it just by sheer will and determination. But why not also stack the cards in your favor and go the extra mile? Why not change into the optimum uniform for the interview? The benefits are greater when we stack the full deck, not just some of the cards in our favor.

Has there ever been a situation when you've felt out of harmony with who you are and what you were wearing? What about when you ran to the store wearing your house cleaning or yard working clothes? What echoes through your mind as you step into the store? *I sure hope I don't run in to anyone I know.* And what usually happens? Yep, not one but two people you haven't seen for a while recognize you.

In that moment, does it feel like an out-of-body experience? Like, what you see is really not who you are? But is that true? You are that person who cleans the house or works the yard, but you're not that person at that moment, standing in the store talking. What we should desire is for people to see us as we are, no more and no less.

If we are truly dressing for success, we should want others to see us as we are and are becoming, not an embarrassed person apologizing for not changing their outfit. Remember, part of the magic of uniform is alignment. If we show up at the store wearing grubby clothes, we have aligned ourselves with being an industrious house worker. At first that doesn't sound too bad, housework is inevitable, and everyone or most everyone must do chores. But at that moment, it becomes your identity—at least for those passing by and taking in first impressions. Once we feel that look from others, it suddenly becomes our identity. Then, an old friend stops us, and we immediately feel disconnected and out of harmony with who we really are. Then the excuses begin. "I apologize for how I look; I was doing chores at home; I normally don't look this way."

Many years ago, when I was single, I tried out one of those online dating sites. I got to know a few ladies online and after several weeks (or maybe it was months) of getting to know them, I narrowed down the likely matches to one, and finally asked her out for coffee. She was ecstatic (I'd like to think), so we picked a time and place.

I dressed in casual yet nice clothes, to reflect my true inner self appropriately. After a few minutes waiting at a table, a lady walked in. I immediately recognized her face—the same face I had seen over several weeks on her bio page. She spotted me and I waved her over. At first glance, my impression took me back. She wore little to no makeup and was dressed in "comfortable" sweatpants and a sweatshirt. These were not stylish exercise clothes. There were no Lulu Lemon brandings in sight. These were gray, old school, ugly sweats.

As she sat down, I asked if she wanted coffee. She replied with a "yes," then added, "I just came from the gym." I thought to myself, *really? This is how you're wanting to make a first impression?* Then I thought, *this coffee date must not be important enough to even wash up for. She could have at least gone to the trouble of dabbing a little eyeliner on or brushing her hair.*

Thank goodness I kept those superficial thoughts well hidden. We ordered coffee, sat back, and had a very nice conversation. As the hour wore on, I sensed her interest in me growing. Still, I couldn't help thinking to myself, *I took this coffee date serious. Of course, you like me, I'm a great guy. A guy who went to the trouble to put himself together—inside and out.* I wasn't trying to be shallow; but my first impression of her was not a very good one. It was a first impression that indicated to me I wasn't significant enough to wrap up her workout thirty minutes before our coffee date.

To finish the story (which I'm sure you're dying to know how it turned out), the date ended and we both walked out the coffee shop, stopped, and faced each other. She shared that she had a very nice time and that she would like to see me again. I responded that it would be nice, or something to that effect. To be honest, I knew I wouldn't call her again. My first impression was simply too strong. So being a schmuck, I led her to believe there would be a call from me in the future. We hugged and then she walked off. After about ten steps, she turned back and yelled, "I clean up really good!" Then she was off.

Clean up really good? I repeated to myself. *Clean up really good?* Why didn't she clean up really good to start with? I wasn't sure what bothered me most about the encounter, the fact that she hadn't gone to any trouble on my behalf or that something didn't feel right.

I hope my embarrassing little story helps to demonstrate how dressing for success can be significant, regardless of the situation. You see, after about fifteen minutes sitting with this lady, I sensed her desire for me growing. She may have been on many of these coffee dates in the past and decided that this would be just like all the others…not worth her time. Only during our conversation did her countenance shift. I could visually see she was genuinely interested in me, but what became more apparent was that she had become acutely aware she was underdressed, and it bothered her. She became more nervous as the hour rolled on.

When we are integrated, we are seldom nervous. I'm not talking about being on-stage nervous, I'm talking about in our normal day-to-day lives. The easiest way to become nervous is to become disconnected with ourselves and lose our integrity. Let your uniform represent you, no matter what the situation is or how many times you have executed the task before—even when meeting for coffee.

Don't Skimp

A few additional points on *dressing for success*. Earlier we covered how people judge us on our appearance, and how thinking they don't is naive. We can wish for the world to be different; we can even adopt an attitude that enlightened people shouldn't care what others think. But just remember, you invested in this book for me to give it to you straight. If people judge us based on our appearance (even if you only accept this statement as partially true), why then would we skimp on our wardrobe?

Note:
If you feel like you have the world by the

> *tail, dress like you do, then others will see that you do.*

If you don't have the world by the tail but want to, dress in such a way that expresses to your inner self your sincerest desires. Make your inner align with your outer and change your outer to reflect your inner.

Now if you want to fast-track your dreams and aspirations, take it to the extreme. Again, I'm not suggesting that you fake it. I'm suggesting that when you affirm what you want, let your outer skin—uniform, reflect your sincerity about it. Uniforms soak through the skin and into your core, creating real tension and transformation to occur. If you don't go to the extreme, you are telling yourself that you're not serious about your goal, dream, desire, or vision. Others will also see that you're not serious. If you don't wear an accurate uniform, others may sense a lack of integrity and see you as a fraud. It's always best to dress in congruency with your true self.

Passion and Vision

Passion and vision are essential elements of high performers. Never be hesitant in letting people see your passion. If you're truly serious about where you're going in life, let it show. That's what dressing for success is all about.

As children, many of us dressed in costumes and uniforms. We pretended to be what we wanted to become once we were older. Friends and relatives saw us. Some may have ridiculed us, even to the point of being brutally rude at times, but others took note. Some relatives and friends encouraged us, supporting our dreams and aspiration. They gave us toys, apparel, or other things that helped reinforce our vision.

When I was young, I wanted to become either a musician or a pilot. I remember holding these occupations constantly in my mind and portraying them with my attire. With every birthday and Christmas, I asked for airplane and music stuff. The reinforcement from my family was incredible, especially from my mom and dad.

Why as adults, do many of us stop dressing up? Most of the time when we do wear a uniform it's because we are obligated to—that is, if we want to keep a job that requires one. Why is it that when we go on a first or second date, we spend so much time preparing ourselves? We choose our attire ever so carefully, then fuss about our hair until we're almost late. Then years later, or for some even months, it seems going to all that trouble is too much bother.

Have we lost our dreams? Do we already have what we need and want, so our goals have little to no pulling power? Have our dreams gone by the wayside along with dressing up? If that is indeed the case and we truly desire to live lives to the fullest and at their zenith, we need to start dreaming again.

What's your vision for the future? Are you on track? What goals do you have for work, for your relationships, and for yourself? When you are clear on these, then tension will start to build in you like it did so many years ago when you were young. Now dress in appropriate uniforms so others can see your passion and your seriousness about your goals and dreams. Most importantly, let the mirror show who you are and what you want to become. Your mind will immediately go to work, making what you see a reality for you.

> **Caution:**
> *You can do too much, too soon, so use sound judgement.*

Use sound judgement. For example, if you desire to be a fireman, I wouldn't suggest you go rent, and wear a fireman's uniform. People may question your psychological health. But what can you do? For starters, join a volunteer fire department and then wear the volunteer T-shirt. Take paramedic classes and wear apparel that signifies you belong and are on your way. Maybe wear a hat that supports the local fire department. There are countless ways to show you're on that journey without doing too much, too soon. Again, use sound judgement. Some goals, desires, and careers will allow for more leniency, while others won't.

We Are the Embodiment of What We Wear

People first see you for what you wear. Even as people get to know you, if you continually dress a certain way, that will become their reality of you. And as we already discussed, it can become your self-fulfilling destiny. Dress sloppy—we become sloppy; dress smartly—we become smart.

If uniforms bring into existence what we become, then let's make our uniform what we intend to become. Most animals can't change their outer shell, fur, or skin. They will always be on the inside what they are on the outside. A leopard is always a leopard; a monkey is always a monkey. But we can change. In fact, we can change several times a day if we want too, and for any number of reasons.

Have you ever been shopping at a store and a stranger comes up to you, thinking you work there? I have. I wondered why they thought I worked there until noticing my shirt color was similar to the actual employees. A couple times I played along, showing them where something was located or answering a question. But there's an easy fix for not being mistaken as a member of that establishment. Don't dress like they do.

Recently I visited a zoo. I came to a part of the zoo where the sign read, *Farm Animals*. The animals I saw beyond the fence were anything but farm animals. Another section had a sign describing a snake. It wasn't a big enclosure. I saw several birds and living things, but no snakes. After a few minutes, I became a little concerned. If the snakes were not in the enclosure, where were they? I began looking around nervously.

My point is, when you look in a gorilla enclosure, you expect to see gorillas. And they're easy to spot—why? Because they're dressed like gorillas. It would be very unusual, and a little alarming, to see a lion dressed as one.

If you want to dress for success, wear uniforms that exemplify success to you—in all areas of your life. If you need to do some research to find the right uniform, then put in the time and do the research. Wear what you want people to recognize you as. No more and no less. Don't lose your integrity. You can remain integrated while dressing for success when you are true to what you are becoming. You don't have to wait until your destination is attained to be congruent. Once you're firmly on the journey, you're becoming what you desire. Your dreams are being fulfilled. Don't wait until you reach a destination to become a winner. Winners are those who set goals and journey towards them. They might fail in the process, but I would still consider their efforts successful when compared to those timid souls who never venture out.

> ***Takeaways:***
> *1. The outer reflects the inner and the inner reflects and perceives the outer. Tend to them both.*
> *2. People will attach an identity to you by what you wear.*

3. Don't fake it until you make it. Be genuinely true to who you are and what you are becoming.
4. Integrity is the cornerstone for achieving success.
5. Affirmation without integrity is telling yourself a fib.
6. Passion and vision are essential elements of high achievers.
7. Don't skimp on your uniform. Go all out.

PERSONAL APPLICATION

Part III

Chapter 7

DRESS FOR WHAT YOU WANT TO BECOME

In the previous section, we discussed having a vision or a goal for what you desire and for every aspect of your life where you're looking to excel and improve. I stated this as the starting point for real transformation. In this chapter, we will dig deeper into goal setting and give examples of how uniforms, properly selected, will boost goal attainment. The takeaways at the end of the chapter will give action steps to begin this process.

Goal Setting

Some of you already have goals and know exactly what you want to obtain and achieve. For others, goal setting may be new. There are many approaches to goal setting. Some approaches are better than others and your personality traits and individual preferences have their place in the selection process. Over the next several paragraphs, I will share and explain the goalsetting process I recommend. It is simple, easy to understand and follow, and it brings results. For those who already have their goals well documented, you may skip to the next section. Let's get started.

Goal Setting Workshop

Goal setting is best accomplished when you have the time to devote to the task and where there are limited distractions. First, grab a lined tablet. One way to immensely improve your success in goal setting is to write them down.

We'll start off with the creative side of the brain. In proper goal setting, it's best to start with the creative side, and then switch to the analytical side.

Before opening your tablet, I want you to close your eyes and take in several deep breaths through your nose. Feel your stomach rise with every breath. Let your chest fall, then your abdomen. Slowly release the air through your pursed mouth. You need to be in a state of mindfulness, one in which you are relaxed; a state where your mind is free from the daily distractions that scream for your constant attention. Keep this technique going until you're in a state of relaxation. Once there, you can open your eyes for the next step in the process.

Now begin thinking about your life. Try to recall the dreams you had as a child. What dreams have you had lately? Try to observe your life as a spectator would. Think about the relationships in your life, your current job, and the work you do. If you don't have a job, what would you like to do? How is your bank account? Your health? How about your happiness and joy level? How about your level of charity, where you give back to the community and serve others? What about your spiritual walk with God? Spend a few minutes visualizing your life.

As a spectator, imagine hovering over yourself at 100 feet. What do you see? Try not to judge at this point. Just let your mind be open and aware of your life up to this point. Can you see yourself as a child? If not, rise up higher, taking in more years of your life. What uniforms have you worn? What "make believe" games have you played? Maybe your upbringing wasn't very pleasant. It doesn't matter for this exercise. What we are searching for is a mind reacquainted with past dreams, struggles, successes, and recent dreams and desires for the future. We will use this information as rocket fuel for goal setting.

Step 1

With your thoughts fresh in mind, we will begin the goal setting process. In Step 1, you will use a pen and paper to document your thoughts. On the sheet of paper, draw a line from top to bottom, dividing the page in half. We will fill out the left side of the page during this step, and the right side in Step 2. Also, we will continue using the creative side of our brains, as this will be a free-flowing exercise.

Hopefully, you have recalled your life over many years and have thought about where life has taken you thus far. Now it's time to think about what you want. Begin by writing down the wants, dreams and desires you recalled as a child. Don't analyze anything as you write, just get your brainstorming thoughts on the paper. Maybe a current situation at work floods your thoughts. Now is the time to write down how you would like it to be. Write as fast as you can. What are your desires? Do you want a new job? If so, where do you want to work, in what field, and doing what? Write it down. What kind of relationships do you want? Do any names come to mind? How would you like these specific relationships to be? Just use a few words for each thought or goal at this point. List them one under the other, leaving the right side of the page open. What would you like your bank account to be? How about your fitness and health? What are you driving? What recreation excites you? In what areas do you want to be competitive? Do you want to live someplace different? Let your mind run free. Write each desire on a separate line. Let all your ideas pour onto the page or pages.

Step 2

Once you're finished, it's time for Step 2. If you're like most people, it didn't take long for you to fill up a page. You may have had to use several pages; if not, that's okay. In Step 2, we will shift our focus toward the reasoning side of our brains, but not completely. That will come in a few minutes.

Let your eyes wander down your list of wants, dreams, and desires. Using a few more words now, describe each one in slightly more detail. Use the space to the right of each want, dream, and desire. This is not an analysis of each item; it's about adding a little more context. This is letting your mind dream a little further on each of your desires. If you had *Pilot* written down in the left column, in the right column you might add: *Commercial Airline, Captain, Southwest Airlines,* if that's your desire. Maybe in the left column it reads *Pickup Truck*. In the right column you might add: *Ford, New, Raptor, Blue*. Finish working down your list.

On your lined paper, you should now have your brainstormed list of wants, dreams, and desires on the left side, and to the right of each one, additional details.

Step 3

Of the wants, dreams, and desires you have written down, it's now time to add a duration for how long they will take to accomplish. This is not when you want to complete the goal, we will add that in Step 4. This is the process time. For instance, a four-year college degree normally takes four years to accomplish. If you wait two years to begin, it will be six years until you are finished, but your actual process time is still four years. If your desire is for a new car, the process time for purchasing a car is rather short, but maybe you'll need to save up money in order to get to the point of purchase. Add that to your process time. This time duration or timeline is just a rough guess that will be used when selecting an actual completion date in Step 4.

Also, be careful trying to determine *how* your goals will be achieved at this point. Let's say it will take five years to be in your new occupation. Your mind might quickly reveal several reasons why you probably can't accomplish that. Push the reasoning aside for a moment and keep this exercise focused on what you think the actual process time is. Use some common sense, but don't overly judge at this point.

Keep your timeline in years to make it simple. In the margin, to the left of each line, add a number 1, for a one-year timeline, 2 for a two-year timeline, and so forth. It's good to have desires and goals that can be reached over several years, not just those taking one year or less. Use these five timeframes: one (year), two, five, ten, and 15 (years) or more. From here on out, we will refer to your desires as goals, for that is what they will become.

Step 4

Now write each of your goals on a separate sheet of paper (you can also use a computer for this section). Underneath each goal, put a date when you would like this goal to be realized. Be specific now. Generality time is over. To turn your ideas and dreams into actual goals, they must become detailed enough for you to see their path to completion.

If a goal will take two years to complete (a process timeline), and you would like to complete it as soon as possible, put a date of completion two years out. If a goal will take one year to complete, but you don't intend to start it for a while, put the date when you would like to complete it, even if it's two, three, or four or more years out. For instance, maybe there's a goal you want to achieve before you retire. Select your retirement date and make the start of that goal plan one year prior if that is appropriate. Of course, you may choose to work it earlier. Step 4 uses a lot of paper and takes a bit of time, but this upfront work, in conjunction with Step 5 will save you an immense amount of time and frustration in the long run.

Step 5

Describe in as many words as necessary, why you want to achieve each goal. I realize doing this step now breaks with the tradition of a lot of goal-setting teachers, however, I have found the earlier this is done, the sooner your gut, emotions, and desire-glands are enlisted. It's good to be very clear about why you want to obtain something, and the earlier the better. If you've picked a goal that really resonates with you, this part of the exercise will be free-flowing and easy. In the process of writing it, you will probably break out in a smile just thinking about becoming this goal or obtaining and having this goal realized. In contrast, you may also find that in trying to write this paragraph, you realize you don't have enough passion for what you've selected. If that's the case, it's better to know now before you put any further effort towards it. If you've identified any that fit in this category, now is the time to discard them.

> *"When you discover your mission, you will feel its demand. It will fill you with enthusiasm and a burning desire to get to work on it."* W. Clement Stone

Step 6

With your paragraphs written out, it's time to prioritize your list of goals. First, bucket your goals according to the desired completion dates you added in Step 4. Bucket your goals one-year out, two-years out, five-years out, etc...

Next, prioritize the goals within each bucket. For example, if you listed winning a golf tournament under your one-year out goals, and also becoming a manger, determine which of these are more important to you. If you have eight one-year out goals, you should have them prioritized one through eight, and the same for your two, five, ten, 15-year and greater goals.

Now review your list. In this part of the exercise, we will focus on your highest priority goals. You can save the remaining goals for another time but let's start with those goals most important to you.

Take the top one or two from each time period until you have a total of six to ten. If you don't have at least six, it may mean there was not enough diversity in your goals. If you try working more than ten, you might find it difficult to focus and complete them all. Keep in mind that these are merely guidelines to help you achieve success. In reality, only you know how determined, and action oriented you are, and how many proverbial irons you can successfully manage in the fire.

Be sure to have a diversity of goals—goals for business, health, sports, exercise, relationships, wealth, spirituality, charity, etc...

Step 7

Now it's time for the largest step, your detailed plans to achieve each goal. Each plan will consist of *all* the details necessary for goal achievement. For plans to be effective they need to be comprehensive. Every task will need to be identified and written out with dates for their completion.

> ***Caution:***
> *Many people stop at this point because it requires a lot of effort to complete. Don't let that be you. Your future success is related to the effort expended.*

Elements of a good plan:
A. Do you need resources to accomplish the goal, e.g., money, investors, bank loans, other people, material, etc.?
B. Do you have the knowledge to complete the goal: e.g., education, degree, skills, etc.?
C. Can you accomplish this alone, or do you need others to help achieve it: e.g., contractors, teachers, mentors, friends, family, or other groups?
D. What will be the hardest aspects in accomplishing this goal? List these as tasks to work through so you'll learn the answers and not become stuck.
E. Identify and list all the actions necessary to discover, become, achieve,

purchase, or obtain this goal. This may result in tens if not hundreds of separate action items, depending on the size of the goal.

Note:
For a quick reference guide on goal setting, see the Goal Setting Steps Worksheet in Appendix A.

Build a plan for each of the prioritized goals you have selected during Step 6. When finished, you will truly have a road-mapped plan for achieving your goals. Before we switch back to our study on uniforms and how uniforms work in partnership with goals, I might suggest a few additional ideas that will help create traction throughout this process.

Print and add your goal sheets to a nice binder so you can review them often. I suggest reviewing them at least weekly, and here's why. First, having your goals continually in front of you and in your thoughts creates a tension and a craving that pulls you towards achievement. Second, I suggest using some sort of daily planner—whether on your phone or in physical form. As you look through your goal sheets each week…pick a specific day that works best…write the tasks/actions that need to be worked for the upcoming week into your planner.

Do this for every task and for every goal according to their schedule. Break these actions out by days as needed. By going to this level of detail and planning, you are eating the elephant one bite at a time. You're also making your highest priority tasks visible so they can be worked as you planned.

Last, I recommend the use of a journal. Journals are great for so many things, especially goal achievement. I recommend you take your journal out each week and document how well you did toward your active tasks and goal achievement—what worked well and what didn't. Where might your plans need adjustment and are there new tasks to be added? Check also for tasks to be deleted. Your journal will document and become your progress report. Use it in conjunction with your goal binder and your daily planner. See the figure below.

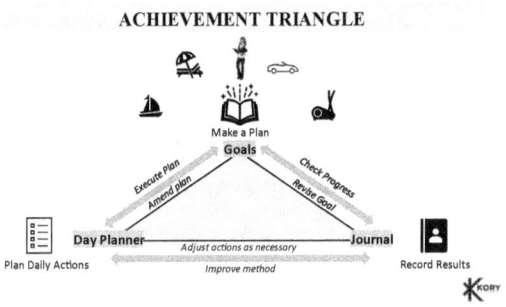

Figure 2: The achievement triangle

Uniforms and Goals

Look over your list of goals and identify how many involve apparel. For instance, if on your goal list you have written, *become a leader in my organization*, what are the leaders wearing in your organization? If on your list you have, *attain a director's position*, what are the directors wearing at your company? Let's say to get in better shape is on your list. What specific exercise did you identify? Yoga? Weight training? Running? What outfit or uniform would cement that image of accomplishment in your mind?

Once you identify the uniform, add it to your plan of action if you haven't already. Even goals where specific attire or uniforms are not applicable may benefit from a second look. For example, let's say your goal is learning to carve wood. Maybe a nice leather, suede, or nylon apron would cement the image of an accomplished woodcrafter into you mind. If so, pick a good one…one that motivates you. Maybe your desire is to learn to cook. As trivial as it may sound, even if you are just cooking at home, ask yourself what your favorite chefs wear on TV. Maybe you don't need a full uniform, maybe a really nice chef's apron or hat will do the trick. What about a new set of professional cutlery?

By enhancing and interlacing your goals with uniforms, you are consciously and subconsciously telling yourself that you are serious. Not every goal has need of a uniform, but for those that do, employing them will amplify your success. Every time you put on your uniform you reaffirm to yourself how serious you are in accomplishing the goal you have written down. It also speaks subconsciously to the child-mind inside you. It reveals you're worthy; you're _____ (professional, expert, ready, accomplished).

Now, What do You Want to Become?

Not only do uniforms declare that you're serious, but they also provide an image for you to live up to. You've no doubt heard the expression, "those are pretty big shoes to fill." Well, choosing the right uniform will become those big shoes for you.

Now it's time to stretch yourself. What do you want to become? What puts a smile on your face when you think about achieving it?

The objective of the chapter, up until this point, is to help you identify and document your goals, dreams, and wishes. Now it's time to strengthen and reinforce them by digging even deeper and releasing any hesitations or ambiguities.

Many people are too conservative when they set goals. They're afraid if they stretch themselves too far, they might fail.

Don't let that be you. Use reality as your guide, but don't sell your dreams and abilities short. Also think about all that you are and do throughout the day. Are you a mom or dad? A high school teacher? Do you play sports? What would communicate to you how serious you are in these areas?

Don't worry about what others may think. Others can pull you back and hold you down. People like to make fun of those who are movers and shakers. Why? Because most people are comfortable when you are like they are. Deep down they don't want you to leave the *group*. Your success may reflect badly on them. Thank goodness not everyone is like that, but when you set goals and start wearing uniforms to establish where you're going in life, those who have settled and given up on higher performance will show up. Count them as they do. Let them be your inspiration that rockets you further and causes you to press-in even harder.

Years ago, I coached boys' soccer. During practices, a few of the boys would show up in serious soccer outfits. They wore the proper shorts, shoes, socks, and shirts. Most of the kids wore soccer shoes, but many didn't go to the trouble of changing out of their school clothes for practice.

It wasn't long before the ones without proper uniforms followed the ones with proper uniforms. It was clear to me as well as the other kids that those wearing the proper soccer attire were serious about learning the game of soccer. Many of those who showed up in street clothes also didn't take the game too seriously. Sure, most wanted to play, but they were unwilling to put forth the effort necessary in practice to be really good. Now, of course, there are exceptions and extenuating circumstances, just like there are in all walks of life. But in general, this example has repeated itself many times and been my observation across a variety of disciplines throughout the years.

When my son was younger, he, used to wear his baseball team coat around even when he wasn't going to and from games. He had a vision of playing baseball at a high level and he wore that vision every chance he could. At times he was chided, even by family members. Years later though, these same family members and friends weren't surprised when he received scholarships to play four years of baseball in college, one year of pro ball in Germany, and an offer to play in Australia. He later took a paying job coaching college baseball. He wore his affirmation every day, and it came true.

How about you? What passions do you have that would benefit from wearing a uniform? Below is a list to get your creative juices flowing.

Passions and Occupations Fit for a Uniform

Cooking
Boating/Boat Captain/Deckhand
Company Manager
Company CEO

- Leader
- Waitress/Server
- Teacher/Educator
- Engineer
- Nurse
- Doctor
- Fitness/Fitness professional
- Coach
- Motherhood
- Fatherhood
- Mentor
- Sports
- Military
- Dock Worker
- Shipping/Warehouse
- Truck Driver
- Racer
- Civic Leader
- Civil Servant
- Clergy
- Pilot
- Craftsman
- Mechanic
- Food Industry
- Mail Service
- Delivery Service
- Writer
- Public Speaker
- Musician/Performer
- Actor/Actress
- Animal Trainer

Animal Caretaker
Healthcare Provider
Gas Station Attendant
Store Clerk

These are only a few suggestions; the actual list for all practical purposes is endless. The more you wear uniforms, the easier it will become at finding relevant and appropriate applications. I've discovered there are really no limits to passion and how wearing a uniform can enhance those passions.

As I wrote the list of passions and occupations fit for uniforms, I reflected on the many times I observed people who took advantage of wearing empowering uniforms...and unfortunately, even more times when people hadn't. So, what is an empowering and proper uniform?

In order for a uniform to become a positive affirmation and for one's dreams and goals to transform them, it's imperative that they know *who they are, what they want, and where they're going*. The integration of these factors is absolutely critical. As with any affirmation, and we are specifically referring to positive affirmations, you must believe with all your heart and mind in your successful outcome.

Writing and reading affirmations should always be done in the present tense as if the affirmation has already come to past. For example, instead of writing, *I will lose 20 pounds,* or *I will become a director at my company,* you should write, *being at my ideal weight* (state what that is) *gives me energy and joy,* or, *leading as a director has allowed me to grow, meet new people, and challenge myself to greatness.*

The key is to connect the future with the present. Your mind will listen to your (future) affirmation in the present and release power to make it so. This is the same principle for why we wear our uniform(s) for what we want to become, the performance level we desire, and the accomplishments we seek. It visually reminds us and others that we are in the present what we seek to become in the future—we are affirming.

Coloring Outside the Circle

What if a person is a trendsetter and desires coloring outside of the proverbial circle? I can't count the number of times I've witnessed employees bucking a recognized dress code. Why? People at their basic core desire individuality. They desire to belong, yet at the same time stand out. People like to be noticed, even introverts to some degree. Some even revel in the attention that distinctiveness brings them. But I won't kid you here. Most of the time when people buck a trend and wear a different uniform than what's in vogue, they do so at the risk of failing. Although doing so at first may give them a bump in significance, most likely it won't to those around them.

It is usually best to model what others in your goal-field are wearing. I say usually because there are times when coloring outside the circle can be beneficial.

Let me share a few cases of people who busted the trend successfully. In each of these cases, coloring outside the circle was an integral part of their journey, and not just because of their uniform. At first, their new trends were not accepted well. It took months, and for many, years to have their new uniforms become an asset and not a liability on their road to goal attainment.

Steve Jobs of Apple made the mock shirt and jeans an iconic business outfit. Once accepted, the new casual look became synonymous with creativity and out-of-the-box thinking. It also transformed the image of the tech industry. Tiger Woods broke through with his own style on the golf course. He made wearing a red shirt and baseball cap a golf essential. Almost overnight, sales of Tiger Woods' branded clothing went through the roof. He broke the long-standing stodginess of golf into a likable and relatable sport. Popularity and viewership exploded.

There are probably examples in your place of business of small trend busters. A manger stops wearing ties and buttons down his shirt. A leader introduces Casual Fridays. Jeans become the symbol of a relaxed environment from one of the female leaders. Even hairstyles can become a trend buster.

In one department I worked, the leaders experimented with the dress code. In the past, the department was known for its stanch attire: suit coats, dress shirts, and ties. One leader announced that suit coats were no longer necessary. A while later, he shared that ties were no longer necessary. He was trying to change the culture into a more modern and engaging one.

Did it work? Not really. Now all the men from that leadership team walked around in button-up white shirts with no ties, and the women wore fewer business suits, but that was all the change effected.

Personally, I feel a white button-up shirt still maintains a stuffy environment. If a relaxed culture is what a group is aiming for, there are far better solutions—and besides, without a tie covering the buttons, it just looks undressed and unprofessional. I changed out of wearing white button-up shirts to wearing mocks. They were proper looking mocks, of course, even purchased at fine stores. Without permission, I started wearing them. I still wore my required slacks, but now instead of a dress shirt, with a couple buttons unfastened, I was bucking the system with mock turtlenecks. No, I was not mocking the system, but it is an interesting play on words.

It wasn't long before my mock shirts were no longer frowned upon. In fact, I noticed several other mangers getting on board with my new uniform. Imitation is always the best form of flattery; after all, I borrowed the look from Steve Jobs. Years later, as my hair was thinning, I decided to wear it short—one-eighth of an inch short. Once people got used to seeing me in short-short hair, the style just became me. Since that day, I've actually had men ask me how I get my hair to look the way it does. Now I'm sure women get asked about hairstyles repeatedly, but men—not so much.

My point is that you can buck the system and make it pay dividends for you, like Steve Jobs and

Tiger Woods, but you need to be very careful and very calculated when doing so. If after walking through the steps described in the next chapter you still believe it's the right move for you, your goal, and your passion, then go for it.

> ***Takeaways:***
> *1. Goal Setting is the beginning of transformation.*
> *2. Document your goals on paper or in digital form.*
> *3. Your past, present, and future dreams hold the keys of your deepest desires.*
> *4. Uniform identification and adaptation should be a part of your goal planning.*
> *5. The understanding of what your heart truly desires is a fountain of life.*
> *6. There are times for coloring outside the circle. Let wisdom guide your path.*

Chapter 8

SELECTING THE RIGHT UNIFORM

Selection Guidelines

Selecting the right uniform is not difficult, but it does require careful thought and planning. In each area of your life, where the application of a uniform makes sense, run through these basic steps to ensure your selection will provide the greatest chances for success. When developing a uniform for business needs, keep in mind that varying day-to-day situations may require different solutions.

Below are guidelines to assist you in your selection process:

Identify your passion necessitating a uniform. This might be from goals you previously had or new goals from the goal setting exercise.

Does your selected area already have a uniform requirement, e.g., fireman, policeman, electrician, restaurant cook, etc.? If so, you may need to follow the requirements for that particular position. That doesn't mean there isn't opportunities for enhancing the uniform, but you will probably need to stay within the prescribed guidelines.

What are successful experts in your desired field wearing? Do a careful study of your desired position, profession, or activity. If your passion is sports related, try to think about what the accomplished athletes wear. Remember, if you're looking to climb the success ladder, look at those who are already two steps, or levels higher.

What could you adopt about these uniforms?

What speaks to you about these uniforms, confirming you're serious about the goal and passion you've selected?

How would this uniform make you feel?

What do you like or dislike about the uniform?

Translate this information into a specific outfit, including accessories. Hold the image of it in your mind's eye until you are clear on what it looks like.

Document the uniform in detail. If it has buttons, how many? If it is a specific color, what color? Does it need accessories or other equipment? Remember the words of Emeril Lagasse, the famous Chef, "Bam! Kick it up a notch" and so should you.

With the new uniform documented, picture yourself wearing it. How does it feel? Don't worry if your mind immediately goes to what your peers might think. They're probably not headed in the same direction you're going anyway. It's okay if the image you're visualizing makes you a little uncomfortable, the uniform affirmation process is not yet complete. There are additional steps necessary in order to bring your dreams into the present, and give your uniform pulling power and magic.

Go to your closet and see if you have all that you need. If not, purchase the clothes, accessories, and equipment that you've documented. Don't rush this process. Make it a special time for you. If you do need to shop, buy yourself an expensive cup of coffee or tea; add in a nice lunch, too. Think about your passion or goal as you carefully select your empowering uniform. This selection and buying process should continue to empower and excite you.

Break the Paradigm.

Over the next couple of chapters, you'll learn how to care for your uniform and the all-important process of dressing and wearing it.

People mistakenly get the idea that dressing for success refers only to a suit and tie or a formal business suit. Please don't fall into this paradigm. Many times, casual wear is the best uniform for the occasion.

> *Success has significance, but transformation changes one's trajectory for a lifetime.*

If a company has a relaxed atmosphere, and the CEO wears jeans or slacks and a V-neck, or jeans and a simple blouse, don't come in wearing a shirt and tie and expect to be promoted.

Additionally, don't be careless about what you wear. Do your homework, remember that your conscious and subconscious mind, as well as those around you, are continuously watching and observing. The one time you head to the store in your pajama bottoms is the time you'll run into someone important.

Note:
Have you considered that maybe your purchases are influenced by what you wear and how your clothing makes you feel?

Selection Criteria Examples

Complete the selection exercise for all the areas of your life where you want increased performance, success, and results.

Below are a couple examples using the selection criteria. The first example highlights a business application and the second one, a non-business application.

Example 1:

Cindy is a goal-setting young lady who desires a promotion at work. She works for a corporate firm where the dress code is casual to semi-formal. As a data entry clerk, she sits with others doing like work in a traditional cubical setting. Most of her peers push the limit on casual attire, and in the past, she has done the same.

Let's read Cindy's answers as she works through the guidelines.

Identify your passion necessitating a uniform.

Cindy: *I want a promotion out of data entry into a lead position or management.*

Does your selected area already have a uniform requirement?

Cindy: *No*

What are successful experts in your desired field wearing?

Cindy: *Two levels up, the men and women are wearing nice slacks and dress shirts. Oh, and they also have physical planners and notebooks they carry with them.*

What could you adopt about these uniforms?

Cindy: *I could easily wear nicer clothes. They wear what I wore when I interviewed for the job a couple years ago. I could use a planner in my current role to help keep track of the action items my lead and boss give me.*

What speaks to you about these uniforms, confirming you're serious about the goal and passion you have selected?

Cindy: *A more formal uniform is required for my desired position, and I would immediately see myself working toward my goal if I dressed the way my supervisor does. I would stand out from my peers.*

How would this uniform make you feel?

Cindy: *It would feel wonderful. I'd be making real changes and taking steps towards what I want, and that feels really great. It would also make me feel special and more ready for a promotion. Currently, I don't think anyone notices me...or my work.*

What do you like or dislike about the uniform?

Cindy: *My lead still dresses sloppy, but our supervisor dresses nicely. I think I will dress more like my supervisor. My inline supervisor is male, but in another department, there is a woman supervisor that's very respected. I like what she wears.*

Translate this into a specific outfit—including accessories. Hold the image of it in your mind's eye until you are clear on what it looks like.

Cindy: *I have the perfect outfit pictured in my mind. I also like the planner the lady supervisor has. I picture myself with one like that too.*

Document the uniform in detail.

Cindy: *Tan slacks with a floral blouse. Both of these I have. I will need a new brown belt and nice brown leather shoes. I will also wear my nice wool coat to work on days when a coat is needed instead of the sweatshirt I occasionally wear. The planner will have a brown leather binder that zips closed. It will be a size that's easy to carry around. I will also take time in the mornings to do my hair. Some mornings, I have to admit, are bad hair days because I sleep in.*

With the new uniform documented, picture yourself wearing it. How does it feel?

Cindy: *I look good. I imagined my peers asking me why I'm dressed up. I think they'll settle down once they get used to seeing me dressing this way. Wearing my new uniform suddenly makes me feel like I have outgrown my current job. I feel like I am truly on my way to getting that promotion.*

Go to your closet and see if you have all that you need. If not, purchase the clothes, accessories, and equipment that you've documented.

Cindy: *I have the stores picked out where I will go to get the shoes, belt, and planner tomorrow. I also selected a special place to have lunch, too. I pulled my slacks and blouse out of the closet. I think I will take them to the cleaners, so they will be perfect for my debut.*

Example 2:

Don enjoys playing racquetball with his fiends after work. He relishes the camaraderie and health aspects of the game, but now he would like to be more competitive. Instead of being driven off the court each game, he decides to take his game more seriously. He sets that as his goal, then selects lessons, affirmations, and uniform as the three major areas of opportunity. This is how Don worked through the ten steps to select his empowering uniform.

Identify your passion necessitating a uniform.

Don: *I want to be competitive at playing racquetball and win.*

Does your selected area already have a uniform requirement?

Don: *No, except my shoes need to be non-marking gym shoes.*

What are successful experts in your desired field wearing?

Don: *Some wear tank tops, and some moisture wicking tops. All of them wear good shorts and nice indoor court shoes. I saw some online that looked really good. They also wear better eyewear then I do; my goggles fog up constantly. Some also have sweatbands around their heads to keep the sweat from running into their eyes.*

What could you adopt about these uniforms?

Don: *I can adopt all of what I observed. I also could upgrade my racket. I'm still using the one I bought in college, and it's pretty beat up. It was a cheap one, but I didn't have much money back then.*

What speaks to you about these uniforms, confirming you're serious about the goal and passion you have selected?

Don: *I think getting the right shoes and a new racket will show me I'm serious about my goal. Also having new glasses will instantly improve my game because I will be able to see clearly. Wearing an outfit tailored to racquetball will help me feel that I'm serious. Being on the court in my workout clothes, including sweatpants hasn't done much to inspire me.*

How would this uniform make you feel?

Don: *Good, like I'm serious and am competitive. It won't be long before I start winning.*

What do you like or dislike about the uniform?

Don: *I like everything about the uniform except some of the shirts I saw. I'm not trying to be a billboard or advertise anything. I think I'll keep my moisture wicking shirt free of advertisements and large logos.*

Translate this into a specific outfit—including accessories. Hold the image of it in your mind's eye until you are clear on what it looks like.

Don: *I got it. This is so cool.*

Document the uniform in detail.

Don: *Okay, my shoes will be black with thin red strips. My shorts and shirt are made from the same moisture wicking material, and the shirt is red, and shorts are black. I saw a red, black, and yellow racquet that would be perfect. Then I would add a simple white headband and expensive antifog glasses. My socks are low cut athletic type—also moisture wicking, and I see myself with a new gym bag—red.*

With the new uniform documented, picture yourself wearing it. How does it feel?

Don: *I feel like a champion. Yeah, my friends are going to make fun of me, but I don't care.*

Wait until they start seeing me win. This is exciting. I really feel like I'm changing already.

Go to your closet and see if you have all that you need. If not, purchase the clothes, accessories, and equipment that you've documented.

Don: *I'll need to purchase everything. I'm going to cancel my game tonight and go shopping instead. I'll treat myself and my wife to a nice dinner out after I shop. I know the best sports store in town. They have everything I need; I already looked on their website to see what they have. To be truthful, I've stopped at this store in the past looking for racket ball gear but always talked myself out of spending the money. I guess I just wasn't ready.*

In these two examples, Cindy and Don gave a mixture of tactical and emotional responses. That was deliberate, the guidelines were constructed to target both. For real transformation to take place, both tactical (mind) and emotional (gut-feeling) changes are necessary. Remember, the *uniform* is to become a part of you—your outer skin. Your uniform speaks volumes to those around you and most importantly, to you, the one wearing it. Let the feelings and the bonding take place. It is the whole process that yields the greatest transformation and results.

One last thing. Your new uniform is there to help you achieve all that you want. It will move you to a new place of courage, confidence, and anticipation of what you desire. **It's not meant to restrict you, it's there to liberate you, boost creativity, and drive passion.**

In addition, the uniform is your armor. No matter who attacks or makes fun of you, you are safe within your armor. Only you know for certain why you're wearing it. It may be an interesting novelty for some. Let them have their offhanded comments, inside your uniform is a person of courage that is about to make history in their chosen field.

> *Takeaways:*
> *1. Select the best and most appropriate uniform to support your goals.*
> *2. Follow the guidelines above and in Appendix B to assist you in your selection process.*
> *3. Make the selection process a continuation of your goal setting activity.*
> *4. When purchasing articles of clothing for your uniform, make it a big deal; keep your motivation and excitement up.*

5. Don't be careless or apathetic when choosing your wardrobe. Be intentional, regardless of whether your uniform is a formal or informal one.

Chapter 9

THE CEREMONY, DONNING THE UNIFORM

To achieve the maximum benefit and effect from wearing a uniform, a detailed ritual is necessary. Time will be required for this ritual; however, it is negligible compared to the benefits one will receive. When practiced for a minimum of 20 consecutive days (or as applicable), the process should become second nature.

The Process of the Under Achievers

Let's begin by reviewing how the majority of people get dressed. We will use an early morning example.

The alarm clock blares its loud music, or worse, the dreaded buzzer. After a series of fumbling and thumping the snooze button, most people slide out of bed and dizzily head to the bathroom. Once the necessities are finished, they turn to the closet and dresser, glassy-eyed, inventorying what's hung, folded, and clean. They might even voice out loud, "What am I going to wear today?"

The clock forces them to hurry, so they hastily grab something they hope matches and suits the needs of the day, then they dress. After a look in the mirror and a glance at the clock, they grab a cup of acid, (coffee) and head off to work.

Now your morning may not resemble the one just depicted, nevertheless, most people rush though the process of dressing. In fact, other than selecting an outfit that matches, people think very little about why they've chosen to wear what they have. Most people miss a golden opportunity to strengthen their goals and bring them into consciousness. Using clothes as affirmations is like popping a power-pill before your activities begin. It's the superhero coming out of the telephone booth, dressed in uniform.

A New Ritual

Now let's examine a new and better process. This new process, or ritual, will assist in bringing your goals into the conscious mind as well as cementing them deep into the subconscious mind, where they can work all day long, steering you toward what you want to achieve. Let's break this ritual process down into steps to make it easier to understand and execute. Once this process has become a habit for all your activities requiring a uniform, then you can modify the process to better suit your unique needs and situations.

Steps for Donning a Uniform

A word of caution before we begin. Although you're free to amend this process to better suit your specific situation, don't rush or shortchange it. This ceremony, or ritual-process, starts your internal transformation. It transports the outer self in, and the inner self out. And one more thing. If you have a morning job or an early activity necessitating a uniform, you may need to wake up ten to fifteen minutes earlier than usual in order to provide enough time for the process steps.

The ritual steps begin with donning a uniform; but that doesn't negate the positive benefits a good shower can provide. A powerful positive mental attitude (PMA) can be accomplished while you wash. Instead of fretting about the day ahead, use your precious time to prime yourself for goal achievement and basking in thankfulness.

Step 1:

Reflect on the activity in which you are about to embark. Are you going to work (job) or to an interview? Maybe you're going to the gym, or perhaps, it's making breakfast at home and then taking your children to school? Whatever it is, meditate on your forthcoming activity.

Step 2:

Bring into your conscious mind, the specific goal you have for this activity. For example: I want to be a high performer at work and obtain a raise and/or a promotion; land a new job; be competitive at racquetball or achieve a particular fitness level at the gym.

Now turn that into an affirmation. I win more than half of the racquetball games I play, I'm healthy and fit and at my ideal weight of 120 pounds. Leading my group allows me to challenge myself and my team to greatness; we exceed all of our unit targets.

Step 3:

Take your uniform, the one you carefully selected earlier, out of the closet. **With each article of clothing, perform a quick mental exercise. Hold the piece in front of you and meditate on its power and purpose.**

The first article of clothing are your undergarments. They are your inner protective barrier. Only you know what undergarments you're wearing, and all day long, you will sense a protective power keeping you safe from harm.

If you wear a standard industry uniform to work, your undergarments may be the only opportunity for adding individuality. The color red may communicate power to you. Maybe you have an important meeting or presentation today and wearing red underwear could signal this extra power all day long. With this extra power you're not afraid. Today you can tackle the tough meeting, job, or interview. Remember, the mind works in creative ways. Red underwear may seem silly, but your mind has a playful childlike aspect to it that will respond. If you don't believe me, try it a few times. Your mind will respond well to fulfilling these notions; and have faith when I tell you, additional power really can be yours.

Use color in your undergarments to give yourself an edge. What's your favorite color? What would wearing that color underneath signify to you? Pick a rainbow of colors and determine what power and energy a particular color holds for you. Maybe its simple tighty-whities that will provide you the feeling you're looking for…a feeling of no nonsense. If that's what you're seeking, then let them communicate that to you all day long.

Step 4:

Now slip on each article of clothing. Recognize how each one embodies your success. As a knight meticulously dons their armor, so should you. With each article feel the protection, energy, power, and determination they give that will propel you towards your goal.
Even if it's just socks, shoes, shorts, and a tank top, go through this process.

You also may want to have some inspiring music playing in the background. Baseball players and wrestlers have entrance or walk-out music, why shouldn't you?

Step 5:

When you're finished dressing, find a mirror, and observe what you see. Align your image to your goal. Synchronize the visual exterior with your goal-seeking interior.

What you're seeking is the fulfillment of your goal reflecting back on you. If you want a specific job—see yourself already having that job. If you want to be proficient at writing—see yourself as a successful writer.

This quick but important step is like hooking yourself up to a high-speed charging station. Feel your power and excitement grow. Don't turn away (or unplug) until you are synched up.

Caution:
Make sure you only think positive reaffirming thoughts. Don't critique yourself. Let others waste time doing that, not you.

Step 6:

This last step is the most important because it uses the first five steps and circulates them throughout the day. It won't do a person much good if after they've stepped away from the mirror, they've forgotten the process they took, the affirmation they're wearing, and the goal(s) they wanted to achieve.

One of the main reasons for going through this process and wearing your affirmation is so it beckons you throughout the day. Every time you see your uniform, remember why you're wearing it.
Dwell on your goal each time you look in a mirror or down at your clothes. Remind yourself that you're moving toward your goal(s). Use your uniform as a mental trigger-point. Every glance should recharge the batteries of your intention.
Don't forget that you're wearing your special undergarments. Smile because they have given you that edge no one else knows about.

Another common mistake people make is not changing outfits for their changing daily activities. Children are notorious violators of this. That's why so many little boys have holes in the knees of their *church*-going pants. Go to the effort of changing your uniform for each major activity you want success in. Don't be casual about this. If you fail to make the effort, your subconscious mind will remind you throughout that activity. And before you know it, your performance will begin to suffer.

It's really quite simple how our mind works. Our mind enjoys and responds to theater. The rise and fall of the affirmed person inside of us influences our reality. What our mind perceives, it believes. Set your character up for success. The mind will go to work turning this image—this theater in our mind into reality.

You might be wondering how long you'll need to utilize this comprehensive ceremony (uniform process); after all, it does take time. The short answer is, how successful do you want to become? The longer answer depends on your unique personality. Some, after a while may find they only need a uniform process infusion from time to time, others may need to stay the course daily for success and happiness. Affirmations only work with repetition followed by action. It's the same with using uniforms to propel you to higher accomplishments, contentment, and happiness.

One last note. If you want to simplify or modify the uniform transformational process for yourself—okay. But don't make this book and teaching on uniforms a fad. A fad is something that comes and goes. If you read this book and try out the process for a few days and then quit, you will never know the power and magic a uniform can hold for you. Stay the course—even if you must amend the process to fit your lifestyle.

> ***Takeaways:***
> *1. To get the most out of your uniform, a methodical ceremony is necessary.*
> *2. Follow the steps above or in Appendix C for the Uniform Ritual (ceremony).*
> *3. Don't be casual. Use the uniform ritual for each of your daily activities.*
> *4. The rise and fall of the affirmed person inside of us influences our reality.*
> *5. Stay the course—even if you must amend the process to fit your lifestyle.*

Chapter 10

TAKING UNIFORMS TO THE NEXT LEVEL

Uniform Care

Up to this point, we have discussed the significance of wearing appropriate uniforms. We have also examined the proper way to don uniforms in order to achieve maximum success. Now we'll explore uniform care.

Believe it or not, there are people who treat their clothes like rags. They throw them on the floor, kick their shoes off or toss them in a pile. But what if clothes could talk? If you asked your clothes how they've been treated lately, what would they say?

Habits affect us greatly, regardless of if they are good or bad. In fact, everything affects us—some things more than others. Our subconscious mind (our built-in personal computer) is recording everything we see, hear, smell, touch, and do. There are some things we have said or have done in our past that are hard to recall. Others are not. Some come back effortlessly into our conscious minds. Whether we can consciously retrieve memories or not, I'm of the belief that they still affect us.

Have you ever felt blue for no apparent reason? Maybe you've been angry or worried about something and didn't know why? I used to get this nagging feeling of worry and unrest, and I couldn't figure out why. Then I stopped listening and watching the news every day. Little did I realize that this negativity machine was slowly dripping acid into my system. I'd wake up each morning with anxiety and worry. Then I discovered *everything* I take in affects me. So, I'm especially careful now to ingest more uplifting and nourishing brain food.

How we treat our clothes—our uniforms, matters too, and will augment or diminish the returns we receive from them. Let's look at a few ways to care for uniforms in order to get the most from them. We'll start with cleaning and folding (or hanging them up). Next, we'll discuss purchasing, then end with accessorizing.

Uniform Cleaning

This section will not be a dissertation on how to launder clothes. If that skill is necessary for you, there are scads of resources, including videos to be had on the Internet. What we will touch on here is the importance of having clean uniforms, and the role that plays in your overall success.

Depending on the type of uniform you wear and how it will be used is key to determining the cleaning method and cleaning frequency. For instance, many companies that require formal uniforms also have or provide cleaning services. If that is the case for you, be sure to take advantage of this service and have the frequency adjusted to meet your needs. Usually in this situation a person is given several uniforms. The uniforms are usually circulated between the cleaners, racks, lockers, or home, and the one that's being worn by the user.

A uniform that consists of a dress shirt, blouse, slacks, or business suit, may require the expertise of a dry-cleaner. For many years I wore dress shirts, slacks, and ties. Early on in that particular career I was tight on money, and so in trying to save a buck, I laundered my own clothes.

I wasn't fooling anybody. I worked hard to clean and press my shirts, but I could never get them to look professionally laundered. It occurred to me one day while wearing a white shirt and sitting next to a man also wearing a white shirt that they weren't the same color. His was white as snow and neatly pressed. Mine? Mine was grayish with subtle wrinkles. My next thought was, could this be why he got a promotion before me? Did my lack of attention in appearance also communicate to my boss how I manage my group? From that day on, I changed my cleaning habits. If I expected to become successful, my uniform needed to show that I was.

Keep your valuable uniform cleaned and pressed. If gym cloths constitute your uniform, change them after every use. And before wearing them again, make sure they are thoroughly laundered. I've known men who, after exercising at the gym, simply remove their dirty gym clothes, wad them up in their gym bag, and pull them out and use during their next training session. Ignoring the obvious noxious odor matter, bacteria can grow rapidly in moist dark environments, and can be a real danger.

Uniform Storage

Take time to fold your clothes properly or pay someone to fold them for you. Consider this another aspect of your uniform ritual. Your uniform is the wardrobe you've carefully selected to be the image of what you desire and want to achieve. Don't be careless when folding and hanging them up. Be deliberate.

Thank the clothes for their part in helping you become successful and happy. Run your hand over them and feel the energy they possess; the energy you gave them when you selected them, the energy you feel each and every time you see them. Buy quality hangers. Straighten out your drawers. Give them the space they need. If other garments that are not part of a uniform infringe upon them, move them. Keep your uniforms special.

Do you know what the term, *throwing in the towel* means? It's used in boxing when one of the sides, representing a boxer, surrenders. It means the fight is over—the bout is stopped; someone has won, and someone has lost. Throwing your clothes on the floor and not folding or hanging them up is akin to throwing in the towel on your goals and dreams. Remember, everything matters. Your mind is recording it all. Treat your uniforms with the respect they deserve.

Uniform Purchase

There are a few things to consider when purchasing uniforms. Like most things in life, you get what you pay for. Now that is not always the case, but more times than not it seems to ring true. Give a teenager a car and it usually ends up being unkempt, unwashed, and in many cases is destined for the salvage yard sooner than it ought. When a teenager purchases their own car, they are much more likely to treat it with care and clean it regularly. Often, they are prouder of it, even though it may not be as new and fancy as the gifted teenager's car.

When we buy cheap inferior clothes, each time we wear them, we are reminded that we had to be cheap and that we weren't worth the extra expenditure…and similar to the car example, we also typically treat them with less care. I'm not referring to buying good clothes on sale or at bargain prices. Getting a good deal is always in fashion.

If you were a soldier in the army and you had to purchase your own uniform, would you opt for the cheapest version or the best? Would a knight say, "I'm on a budget, give me the thinnest metal you have please?" I doubt it. He would want the best protection—at any cost.

Select your wardrobe wisely. Pick clothes that convey how special and valuable you are. Purchase clothes that radiate your goal and destiny. Every time you glance at them, it should bring a smile to your face and confidence to your step. Going cheap simply doesn't have the same effect.

Make sure your uniform fits. Don't buy something that brings out a presumed flaw. You want to draft power every time you view your uniform, not weakness and judgement. Several times, I have purchased one size larger or smaller just to save a buck when the proper size wasn't on the sale rack. In each case I ended up regretting that decision. I guess I was a slow learner.

Accessorizing

Another factor to consider when creating a uniform is accessorizing. Accessories and equipment can add distinctiveness to a uniform in addition to increased usefulness. Accessories can even be things unseen or unknown to anyone except the wearer. Even a pocket-sized package of tissue can hold a unique sense of purpose. Below is a list of accessories, flair, and equipment that may be useful in rounding out your special uniform.

>Pocket knife
>Money clip
>Wallet or card holder
>Purse
>Unique key ring
>Belt
>Tie clasp
>Necklace(s)
>Earrings
>Bracelet(s)
>Exclusive and unique socks
>Hat
>Helmet
>Scarf
>Coat
>Pocket pill containers
>Daily planner
>Briefcase
>Duffle bag
>Gym bag
>Gym accessories
>Gloves
>Pens and mechanical pencils
>Folders
>Notebook

Journal
Umbrella
Rings
Pocket protector
Cuff Links—yes, they are still used
Backpack
Unique and special water bottle
Coffee and/or Tea Cup
Lunch box or bag
Address book
Phone
Phone-case
Bluetooth ear bud(s)
Headband
Hair ties
Pictures
Pins and buttons
Work specific tools
Pads (knee, shoulder, etc.)

There really is no end to the number of accessories and equipment one could select. Choose items that would enhance the look, feel, and use of your uniform. Give your subconscious mind a bit of theater. And one last point, don't discount what sentimental objects can do for you.

There are days when I wear a cross under my shirt. Every time I feel the cold metal against my chest, I send up a prayer, knowing that God is with me. Another item I often carry is a small pocketknife that was my father's. Just having it with me gives me an edge. Brides wear something old, something new, something borrowed, and something blue. Think about what items you have or could obtain that might raise your self-confidence and goal-seeking mindset.

> ***Takeaways:***
> *1. Treat your uniform with respect.*
> *2. Keep you uniform laundered and put away for the next use.*
> *3. How we treat our clothes—our uniforms, will augment or diminish the returns we receive from them.*
> *4. Purchase quality, you will never regret it.*
> *5. Accessorizing can turn a satisfactory uniform into a remarkable one.*
> *6. Make your uniform practical, like a multi-tool pocketknife.*

TEAM AND BUSINESS APPLICATION

Part IV

Chapter 11

VOLUNTARY UNIFORMS

Uniforms can be extremely powerful when implemented in groups and organizations. They can also have the opposite affect if implemented incorrectly. Uniforms can aid in the motivation of teams, support synergy between workers, and present a professional and identifiable appearance to customers.

Team uniforms are either adopted voluntarily or mandated like they are in the military and various other trade professions. Whether voluntary or mandatory, a uniform can be a positive addition to any group. In this chapter, we will focus on voluntary uniform adoption. In the following chapter we'll examine mandatory uniforms and their usage.

Voluntary Uniforms

A number of years ago, I implemented a High-Performance Organization (HPO) initiative at an aerospace company. The purpose of the initiative was to break a larger team (about 700 employees) into smaller high-powered groups and give them autonomy over their portion of the business. During the implementation, an interesting trend occurred. I was asked by several of the teams if they could procure teamwear, or uniforms. I wholeheartedly approved and paid for any team willing to do so. It was also interesting to note the maturity of the teams that came to me for this request.

Teams didn't ask for uniforms on day one. It took working through the initial phases of the program before they were ready, and in a position to be identified with the team's mission and other team members. As teams reached higher phases, they were noticeably different. Not long after embracing uniforms, they developed into self-empowered teams, fully enrolled in their team's mission and objectives, and needing very little guidance and oversight from their direct manager.

Isn't it interesting how one doesn't need to coerce someone to wear a shirt, hat, or jacket from their favorite sports team or musical band? "What beer do you drink?" Oh, I see it's printed on your shirt. "What political persuasion are you?" Oh, it's written on your hat. Why? As we noted earlier, it's the need for affiliation. We all have a deep desire inside us to be a part of a larger group. We are social creatures. Birds of a feather flock together, and uniforms help us to do just that. They help satisfy this human need.

If you were/are privileged to wear a military uniform from one of the several branches, you became/are one with the greater service brotherhood and sisterhood. Have you ever worn a team jersey of an opponent to a home game? Immediately the home team fans, decked in their home team colors, becomes a unified group against you. They may not know anyone around them, but because they are wearing the right colors and you aren't, you are the outcast.

Uniforms are powerful. It's almost frightening to realize just how powerful they are. Our goal in this chapter is to learn how to harness that power to accelerate teams into greatness. What is greatness? In this connotation, it is individuals operating as one cohesive unit. A team, when operating as one powerful unit can succeed in dimensions and results far faster and to a greater extent than the sum of the individuals combined.

Creating a Voluntary Uniform Culture

The greatest challenges for any organization are in the areas of culture and environment. Should one want uniformity and camaraderie, culture needs to be nurtured and made a priority. Culture isn't an implementation, and it isn't a program, although too many leaders believe it is. A healthy culture stems from a well-nourished and led environment.

Think of a garden. In order to have a bountiful growing garden, you must put in the time and work. You must carefully prepare the soil, plant the seeds, water judiciously, and then tend to the weeds as they begin their assault on your invested efforts. It's the same with an organization's environment. If treated and cared for like a garden, a healthy culture can grow, and with it, opportunities for teams to flourish and self-identify with one another and with the organization.

In an environment that has been carefully cultivated, anyone can suggest adopting a uniform. It can be a request from inside the team, or it can come from one of the leaders. If the culture is right, suggesting a uniform from leadership won't be an issue. If there is a lot of pushback, it's possible that the culture is not ready or isn't pervasive throughout the organization. One or more teams may possess a great culture, but the environment is not fertile enough to affect the entire organization—especially if leadership is still regarded as outsiders. Remember, this is supposed to be voluntary. If a leader suggests using uniforms and it plops, the leader should move on and focus their attention on cultivating the environment.

One additional note. It's a reasonable sign of cultural maturity when teams internally decide to implement uniforms or team-wear. This isn't always the case; some mature teams do benefit from a little external prompting of ideas.

Implementation

When a team decides to adopt uniforms, the use of carefully constructed guidelines or a policy will assist them in consistency and clarity. This will also help new members in the future.

If leadership has specific guidelines, requirements, and needs the team must consider before uniform selection, leadership should give this information to the team early so their uniform can be built around it. A real motivation killer is giving a team autonomy and then taking it away with rules and regulations after the fact.

Make sure requirements are provided openly, quickly, and with inclusivity. The team should not have resistance if done in this manner. If a team works in an environment where dressing in tank-tops create a safety concern, help them understand why this type of uniform is unsuitable.

The question of who pays for the uniforms or team-wear depends on the situation. If it is a recreational softball league, each player may choose to pay for their own. If it is a team inside a business, that business may decide to cover all the expenses. If not, individuals within the organization might choose to pay the costs. Many times, a reward system is initiated, with objectives and targets established. When teams reach the specified target(s), uniforms, or articles of a uniform (like jackets) can be used for reward. This positive affirming method can work wonders in the right setting. Many people and teams will do incredible things for visual recognition. Take soldiers; they will work hard, even risking their very lives at times to add sashes, badges, buttons, and pins. But it's really not about the flair, it's what the flair represents, and so it is with a uniform.

One additional thought on costs. A uniform (or team-wear) doesn't need to be expensive to be effective. Matching shirts or hats can go a long way in helping with esteem, camaraderie, and performance. I've observed even small somewhat insignificant accessories facilitate transformational qualities, like patches, stickers, matching tool totes, and even pocket protectors. There are as many uniform solutions as there are teams and groups; and many of the solutions won't require CFO approval.

Application

Voluntary uniforms are…after all, voluntary, and yet as we discussed above, can be quite advantageous. If you think an application seems fitting in your situation and you'd like to propose the use of uniforms, see how the rest of the team responds. Carefully studying their reactions will let you know where they are on the team's cultural journey. Maybe the application isn't suited for a complete uniform but don't give up. There may be another uniform solution the team could adopt.

If it's for a team sport, implementation may come easy. Other applications may take considerably more work, and extreme patience may be needed for those desiring to change the paradigm.

You might also look for different ways to enhance camaraderie and team cohesiveness. I once had a team of diverse managers who led very different groups. I bought them fancy leather folders embossed with our company logo. Before long, and without even a plea, each of these leaders carried their special folders wherever they went during working hours. One could spot a leader from my organization just by noticing the unique folder they carried. The leaders were also very appreciative of the gift and gesture, and it helped bring our diverse team a little closer.

> ***Takeaways:***
> *1. We have a deep desire to be a part of a larger group.*
> *2. Uniforms can be an aid in bringing about cohesiveness.*
> *3. A team, when operating as one powerful unit, can succeed in dimensions and achieve results far faster and to a greater extent than the sum of the individuals combined.*

4. The greatest challenges for any organization are in the areas of culture and environment.
5. In an environment that has been carefully cultivated, anyone can suggest adopting a uniform.
6. It's a reasonable sign of cultural maturity when teams internally decide to implement uniforms.
7. When a team decides to adopt uniforms, the use of carefully constructed guidelines or a policy will assist them in consistency and clarity.
8. It's not about the uniform; it's what the uniform represents that is so powerful.

Chapter 12

MANDATORY UNIFORMS

Steps and Considerations

There are countless businesses that require uniform use. Many of these businesses fall into the trades and services bucket, and there are a number of reasons for this. Many companies deal with regulatory requirements, making uniforms compulsory. Some adopt uniforms because of safety concerns while others as a result of various working environments. Clean room environments require a different uniform solution than those whose work deals in filthier environments. And some businesses require uniforms strictly for company branding and recognition.

At companies with an already established uniform policy, there's usually less impediments for adaptation and compliance. That's not to say there aren't still challenges. The 80/20 rule in many cases is alive and well. In all walks of life, a percentage (roughly 20%) of individuals will push the boundaries, and for these, uniform adherence will be a problem.

At times additional measures from management will be needed to ensure compliance. I won't spend too much time on these individuals only to make you aware that this is a reality, and if you are in management, it will need some attention. Thankfully, it is usually only a small percentage (~20%) of the team. However, spending too much time supervising them may keep you from more important tasks and priorities and your larger (~80%) compliant team. Still, when dealing with regulatory requirements, offenders must be managed appropriately.

At FedEx, seatbelt use is mandatory. Their trucks are fitted with brightly colored orange seat and shoulder belts. FedEx representatives driving in the vicinity can easily spot noncompliant drivers, take note, and address the situation. Military, as well as other industries, have uniform inspections. Even in baseball, uniforms (including personal protection) are checked. In the electrical power industry, many parts of the uniforms are continuously checked to ensure arc-flash and shock arresting capabilities meet strict regulatory requirements. There are even parts of uniforms that are sent to specialists to be inspected and certified.

There are also constructive approaches to uniform compliance. Instead of penalizing poor uniform adherence, adopt a reward system as an alternative solution. In the end, you may need to find an approach that works best for them, and it may be a combination of methods.

Share the Reasons

Reasons drive behavior. Whether the uniform is a regulatory requirement or a company requirement, people respond better when they have the facts and can resonate within themselves the reasons and benefits for adopting the uniform policy. Even if the uniform is solely to present a unified company image, sharing the reasons why the company feels this is important will go a long way towards gaining compliance.

Requesting Input

Another great way to achieve compliance is to seek input before finalizing the uniform. Many companies select a small subset of employees to research and select options for the proposed uniform. The company leaders might start by giving the group a list of requirements as a baseline or empower the team to research the job needs and any regulatory or safety requirements before beginning the uniform selection process.

Once the requirements for the uniform are established, the team will select multiple sample uniforms, usually from several vendors or suppliers, and evaluate them. The team will typically choose the top two to four options, and then obtain management approval. With approval in hand, the team requests each supplier to provide sample uniforms in their business colors and with their company logos applied if feasible. When all the samples are in hand, the team will display these for all the employees to view and vote on.

Selecting uniforms in this manner has proven successful for many companies. Getting early input from those who will actually be wearing them is the key. Even when management provides a set of requirements in the beginning, if the process is carried out correctly, the team will still be able to feel autonomy, allowing for complete ownership and buy-in at the user level.

> *Caution:*
> *Too many companies implement uninspiring and unempowering uniforms. Nobody wants to look hideous, even when repairing a large generator. While having only a manager and a trusted employee select the uniform may be the quickest method, it's usually not the best. Don't do your team and company a disservice by being too hasty. Do all you can to enroll as many of the end users (wearers) as possible. Being creative and expending the time upfront will pay huge dividends both for you and your employees.*

Do They Need to be Identical?

Do all the uniforms need to be identical? The answer to this question is maybe. It really depends on the business and application. There are many businesses where employees have a selection of uniforms to wear. If it's cold, they can wear a warmer version, e.g., sweater, coat, long pants, etc... A company might have a range of offerings to meet both the company's needs as well as the employees' desire for individualism. Some companies utilize unique uniforms for varying applications and roles. Using this method, one can rapidly identify individuals from a needed team or group. Others adhere to one uniform style for all positions, regardless of roles. Determining what's best for your application will depend on the factors that are important to you, and your company.

> *Takeaways:*
> *1. Reasons drive behavior.*
> *2. Many companies deal with regulatory requirements, making uniforms compulsory.*
> *3. When dealing with uniform regulatory requirements, compliance is mandatory and should be managed appropriately.*
> *4. Sharing the reasons why your company believes uniforms are important will go a long way towards gaining compliance.*
> *5. Getting early input from those who will actually be wearing them is the key.*
> *6. Do all you can to enroll as many of the end users (wearers) as possible when selecting uniforms.*

Chapter 13

UNIFORM POLICIES

When implementing and employing uniforms, leadership should first ensure a uniform policy exists; and if it does, is it comprehensive enough to serve the company and employees effectively? Once, after a modest amount of research and consideration, it may be necessary to create a new policy or significantly revise the existing one.

Some companies may determine they no longer have a need for mandatory uniforms. Others may choose to go back through a more engaging process and update their uniforms and policy. Some companies are in the beginning stages of their uniform journey and will need to establish a policy that serves the team and company.

Components of a Good Uniform Policy

A good uniform policy should empower employees, delineate regulatory requirements, and outline company objectives and needs. To accomplish this, the policy will need to be comprehensive. Rushing to put a policy in place will most certainly result in rework and revisions later.

Let's cover the components of a good uniform policy. These will be generic in nature; your policy may require more or less information depending on your specific application and business needs. The example here is business-related, although a non-business policy is created in much the same manner.

Policy Components

(A) Governmental matters:
Company name
Date created, including revision records
Person(s) or group maintaining the document
Effective date of policy

(B) Synopsis items:
Organization, group, team, and employees affected by the policy
Policy summary

(C) Policy details:
Uniform description
Uniform use—when and how the uniforms

are to be used, including seasonal considerations
Regulatory requirements
Safety equipment
Miscellaneous accessories and equipment
Uniform care and cleaning, including cleaning service details if applicable
Procurement and renewal information
Storage considerations and information, (also if onsite storage is provided)

(D) Frequently asked questions:

(E) Policy authority and approval signature(s):

(F) Revision process:

Note:
It's generally a good idea, as trends, designs, and new materials change, to refresh uniforms on a regular and scheduled basis. This doesn't mean every year, but consideration should be given to meet employee as well as business needs. For instance, football team uniforms begin losing their splendor if they are not frequently updated. It's fascinating how energized a previously poor performing team can become with new uniforms—not to mention their fan base.

Policy Writing

Similar to selecting uniforms, stakeholders should be involved when writing the uniform policy. Just as uniforms that are chosen by management and decreed to the masses lack empowerment, so will policies without employee and stakeholder involvement fall flat. Have the team select a subset of members to work with leadership as necessary to create, modify, and write the uniform policy. Even recreational softball teams will benefit from using this method.

Policy Communication

A policy holds little value if it isn't read and understood. Be sure to make the policy an annual read for all stakeholders. Incorporating a signature page or an online checklist is typically a good idea. Likewise, annual reading of all company policies is just good practice. Having knowledge of what, why, when, where, and how, contribute to stakeholder enrollment.

Takeaways:
1. A uniform policy should empower employees, delineate regulatory requirements, and outline company objectives and needs.
2. Stakeholders should be involved when writing the uniform policy.
3. Have the team select a subset of members to work with leadership as necessary to create, modify, and write the uniform policy.

4. A policy holds little value if it isn't read periodically and understood.
5. Having knowledge of what, why, when, where, and how, contribute to stakeholder enrollment.

Chapter 14

CONCLUSION

Summary

If you've made it to this point, you've no doubt learned the power and efficacy uniforms hold. You've learned that uniforms are more than just cloth and accessories, wrapped around a person. For uniforms to generate their magic, the wearer must be transformed from the inside out and from the outside in.

Observers of those in uniforms react more favorably when they are convinced the wearer is congruent. Put another way, the uniform wearer's outside reflects their inside and their inside is reflected on their outside. We revealed this earlier as having integrity.

Uniforms really can take you, your team, and your organization to heights never before believed possible. Having a clear vision of what you want is powerful. Using goals to capture your vision puts fuel in your tank. Stepping into your goals by affirming them and wearing a uniform takes your goals off the paper and places them onto the launching pad. Then as you use the uniform transformation process, your goals are ignited, and like a powerful rocket, will propel you to the stars, where virtually nothing can get in the way.

It all starts with a commitment to transform yourself, your team, or your organization. Wearing a uniform is an action step. Action steps are vital if one is serious about becoming more and achieving at their highest potential.

Throughout this book, I have never stated a person can't achieve what they want or go where they want to go if they don't adopt a uniform transformation process. I also never stated that it is possible to win the lotto or guess the right horse at the track; however, I wouldn't trust my future prosperity, livelihood, and happiness on either of these approaches. For most of us, some form of uniform transformation process is necessary for true success, even if it's not articulated and detailed as thoroughly as it is in this book.

There are business leaders who wear white shirts every day to the company office. Why? Because they prefer a simpler uniform. They say it frees up their creative juices to focus on more important tasks and goals. For some, such a simple uniform holds little transformational power. They might make it to the launching pad, but there may not be enough fuel to blast them skyward. Some uniforms are simple and supportive, others need to be more elaborate and intentional to be effective.

Let your uniform impart to others that you are serious about your passions. Let it communicate to you all day long, bolstering your confidence for winning and succeeding, with its inaudible and persistent prompting.

Next Steps

If you don't have your goals clearly written out, return to that section of the book and begin the goal-setting exercise.

Go through your goals and your daily, weekly, and monthly actions and activities. Identify all the areas where adopting the uniform transformational process will benefit you.

If you're a leader of an organization, carefully consider if a formal uniform makes sense for one or more of your teams.

Go through your closet and identify your empowering and disempowering clothing.

If you're a leader, observe what your team wears on a daily basis and determine if it is empowering them to greatness?

Go shopping if needed. Have fun creating your physical affirmation.

Start a uniform ritual. Good habits not only foster a successful life for us, but they can also influence those around us and the teams we're associated with.

Go back through this book. Once is not enough to harvest all the information detailed here that would bring you maximum benefit.

Start today. If you had a pot of gold, wouldn't you be excited to put it to good use?

Let your uniform transform you from the outside in and the inside out.

Don't be casual about what you wear ever again. If you are truly serious about making real progress in your life, your teams' life, and your organization's...stay the course.

Final Thoughts

Happiness is a fickle thing. All of us desire to be happy, whether at home, at work, or wherever we are. Happiness is also not found when we finally reach the top of the mountain. Maybe we will receive a short burst of satisfaction from an accomplishment, but that quickly fades as the next mountain appears and beckons us onward. If we hold off being really happy until we reach some finite level, we may never be truly happy. In fact, we may become extremely despondent.

We've probably all heard it said that happiness is not the destination but in the journey. I will echo that resolve. The point is, there is no pinnacle or objective that will genuinely satisfy you once you've achieved it. The truly happy person understands this and lives their life in the present, while growing and becoming all they can be as they travel along life's journey. And this meaning of happiness does not have a level or date stamp on it. *I call this living at one's pinnacle, not at the pinnacle.*

Goals, affirmations, and uniforms can pull the future in close. This allows us to ensure the feeling of success every day along our journey. The smile you share with others should be just as wide on the day of your first step as when you reach one of your ultimate goals.

Have fun selecting your uniforms. Enjoy how they make you feel. Recognize that you're already what you want to become. Don't put your career, your success, your love, your passions, or your life on hold. Every day is a new beginning—a new opportunity to live life at your pinnacle. Let your inner child relish the theater you have created. It will spur you to greatness and spur your happiness every day.

I wish you all the success in life as you and your teams are transformed by the magic which is uniform.

Adventure Courageously

Appendix A
Goal Setting Steps

Step 1:
- Draw a line on a piece of paper from top to bottom, dividing it in half.
- Write down your wants, dreams, and desires on the left side of the paper using as few words as possible.
- Write as fast as you can, listing each one under the previous one on a separate line. This is a brainstorming exercise to get as many of your thoughts on the paper as possible.

Step 2:
- Using additional words, describe in slightly more detail on the right side of the paper each of your wants, dreams, and desires documented on the left side.
- Do this for each line, adding more context to your initial brainstorming list of items.
- If you had *Pilot* written on the left side, to the right on the same line you might add: *Commercial Airline, Captain, Southwest Airlines.* If you had *Pickup Truck* listed to the left, in the right column you might add: *Ford, New, Raptor, Blue*.

Step 3:
- Write the process time (timeline) it will take to accomplish each of your wants, dreams, and desires in the margin to the left.
- This is not a completion date; this is the time it takes to accomplish the goal. For instance, getting a four-year degree usually takes four years. The process time for purchasing a car may at first seem short, but if you need to save up the money first, your timeline will be much longer.
- Be careful trying to determine *how* your goals will be achieved at this point. Keep this exercise focused on what you think the actual process time will be. Use some common sense, but don't overly analyze at this point.

- Keep your timeline in years to make it easy. In the margin to the left of each line, add a number—1, for a one-year timeline, 2 for a two-year timeline, and so forth.
- It's good to have desires (goals) that can be achieved over several years, not just those taking one or less. Use these five timeframes: one, two, five, ten, and 15 years or greater.

Step 4:
- Write each of your goals on a separate sheet of paper (you can also use a computer for this section).
- Underneath each goal, put a date on when you would like this goal to be realized. If a goal takes two years to complete (process timeline), and you would like to complete it as soon as possible, put a date of completion two years out. If a goal takes one year to complete, but you don't intend to start on it for a while, put a date when you would like to complete it, even if it's two, three, or four or more years out.
- This step uses a lot of paper and takes a bit of time, but this up-front work, in conjunction with Step 5 will save you an immense amount of time and frustration in the long run.

Step 5:
- Under the date of completion for each goal, describe in as many words as necessary, why you want to achieve this goal.
- Do this for each separate goal-sheet.
- It's good to be very clear about why you want to obtain something.
- If you've picked a goal that really resonates with you, this part of the exercise will be free-flowing, easy, and fun. If you find in writing this paragraph that it is a struggle, you might realize you don't have enough passion for what you've selected.
- If you've identified goals lacking your passion, discard them now.

Step 6:
- Bucket your goal-sheets according to the desired completion dates you added in Step 4.
- You goal-sheets should be grouped in one-year out, two-years out, five-years out, etc...
- Prioritize the goals within each bucket or grouping. For example, if you listed winning a golf tournament under your one-year out goals, and also becoming a manger,

determine which of these are more important to you. If you have eight, one-year out goals, you should have them prioritized one through eight, and the same for your two, five, ten, and 15-year and greater goals.
- Take the top one or two from each time frame until you have a total of six to ten. If you don't have at least six, it may mean there was not enough diversity in your goals. If you try working more than ten, you might find it difficult focusing and competing them all.
- Be sure to have a diversity of goals, e.g., business, health, sports, exercise, relationships, wealth, spirituality, charity, etc...

Step 7:
- Build a plan to accomplish each of your prioritized or down-selected goals.
- Each plan will consist of all the details necessary for goal achievement.
- For plans to be effective they will need to be comprehensive.
- Every task will need to be identified and written out with dates for their completion.
- Elements to a good plan are:

  A. Do you need resources to accomplish the goal, e.g., money, investors, bank loans, other people, material, etc.?

  B. Do you have the knowledge to complete the goal, e.g., education, degree, skills, etc.?

  C. Can you accomplish this alone, or do you need others to help achieve it, e.g., contractors, teachers, mentors, friends, family, or other such groups?

  D. What will be the hardest aspects of accomplishing this goal? List these as tasks to work through, so you'll learn the answers and not become stuck.

  E. Identify and list all the actions necessary to discover, become, achieve, purchase, or obtain this goal. This may result in tens if not hundreds of separate action items, depending on how big the goal is.

Appendix B
Uniform Selection Guidelines

Step 1: Identify your passion necessitating a uniform.

Step 2: Does your selected area already have a uniform requirement?

Step 3: What are successful experts in your desired field wearing?

Step 4: What could you adopt about these uniforms?

Step 5: What speaks to you about these uniforms, confirming you're serious about the goal and passion you've selected?

Step 6: How would this uniform make you feel?

Step 7: What do you like or dislike about the uniform?

Step 8: Translate this information into a specific outfit, including accessories. Hold the image of it in your mind's eye until you are clear on what it looks like.

Step 9: Document the uniform in detail.

Step 10: Picture yourself wearing it. How does it feel?

Step 11: Go to your closet and see if you have all that you need. If not, purchase the clothes, accessories, and equipment that you've documented.

Appendix C
The Uniform Ritual

Step 1: Reflect on the activity in which you are about to embark.

Step 2: Bring into your conscious mind the specific goal you have for this activity, then turn it into an affirmation.

Step 3: With each article of clothing, perform a quick mental exercise. Hold the piece in front of you and meditate on its power and purpose.

Step 4: Now slip on each article of clothing. Recognize how each one embodies your success. As a knight meticulously dons his armor, so should you. With each article, feel the protection, energy, power, and determination it gives that will propel you towards your goal.

Step 5: When you're finished dressing, find a mirror, and observe what you see. Align your image to your goal. Synchronize the visual exterior with your goal-seeking interior.

Step 6: Dwell on your goal each time you look in a mirror or down at your clothes. Remind yourself that you're moving toward your goal(s). Use your uniform as a mental trigger-point. Every glance should recharge the batteries of your intention.

Appendix D
Resources

The following are books, websites, and other media related to the subjects examined throughout the book and are provided for those desiring a more in-depth study on the specific topics.

Chapter 1

French Military Uniforms: Napoleonic French Military Uniforms 1798-1814: As Depicted by Horace and Carle Vernet and Eugène Lami (From Reason to Revolution) - Guy Dempsey, *Helion and Company*, November 15, 2021.

Early Uniforms: An Illustrated Encyclopedia of the Uniforms of the Roman World: A Detailed Study of the Armies of Rome and Their Enemies, Including the Etruscans, Gauls, Huns, Sassaids, Persians and Turks - Kevin F. Kiley, *Lorenz Books*; Illustrated edition, February 16, 2013.

Chapter 2

Early Sports Uniforms: Antique Sports Uniforms & Equipment: Baseball, Football, Basketball 1840-1940 - Dan Hauser, *Schiffer Publishing*, October 20, 2008.

Chameleons: Chameleon - Laurie Vitt, *Britannica*, https://www.britannica.com/animal/chameleon-reptile

Chapter 3

Judging: 10 Reasons to Stop Judging People - Barbara Markway Ph.D., *Psychology Today*, October 24, 2014, https://www.psychologytoday.com/us/blog/living-the-questions/201410/10-reasons-stop-judging-people

Law of Attraction: Think and Grow Rich - Napoleon Hill, *Tarcherperigee*, August 18, 2005.

Affirmations: Positive Imaging: The Powerful Way to Change Your Life - Norman Vincent Peale, *Ballantine Books;* Reissue edition, August 27, 1996.

The New Psychology of Winning: Top Qualities of a 21st Century Winner – Denis Waitley, *G&D Media*, May 25, 2021.

Chapter 4

Transformation: Unleash the Power Within: Personal Coaching to Transform Your Life! (Audio CD) – Tony Robbins, *Simon & Schuster* Audio, April 7, 2020.

Group Think: Groupthink – Author Unknown, *Psychology Today,* https://www.psychologytoday.com/us/basics/groupthink

Chapter 5

Perception: Understanding the Secrets of Human Perception – Peter M Vishton, *The Teaching Company*, January 2011.

First Impressions: The First 15 Seconds of Your Job Interview Might Decide the Outcome - Maureen Reese, *Lucas Group*, November 26, 2019, https://www.lucasgroup.com/your-career-intel/first-seconds-interview-decide-outcome/

First Impressions: The 42 Laws of First Impressions to Create Lasting Impact in Business and Life - Max Noble, *Beyond Publishing*, January 29, 2018.

Modeling: Unlimited Power – Anthony Robbins, *Nightingale Conant* (audio), January 1, 1986.

Connection and Dopamine: Understanding Dopamine: Love Hormones And The Brain - Abigail Boyd, *Better Help*, February 24, 2020. https://www.betterhelp.com/advice/love/understanding-dopamine-love-hormones-and-the-brain/

Affinity: Create a Sense of Belonging - Karyn Hall, Ph.D, *Psychology Today*, March 24, 2014. https://www.psychologytoday.com/us/blog/pieces-mind/201403/create-sense-belonging

The Ugly Duckling: Story - Hans Christian Andersen, *New Fairy Tales. First Volume - C. A. Reitzel*, 11 November 1843.

Chapter 6
How to Succeed in Business Without Really Trying: Movie (Production Company *Mirisch Corp.*, Distribution Company *United Artist March 9, 1967)*: Based on the musical "*How to Succeed in Business Without Really Trying*," music by Frank Loesser,

book by Abe Burrows, Jack Weinstock and Willie Gilbert (New York, 14 Oct 1961), which was based on the book "*How to Succeed in Business Without Really Trying; the Dastard's Guide to Fame and Fortune*" by Shepherd Mead, *Simon and Schuster*, (New York) January 1, 1952.

Chapter 7

Envy: Why It Doesn't Feel Good When Someone Else Succeeds - Robert L. Leahy Ph.D., *Psychology Today,* April 12, 2018. https://www.psychologytoday.com/us/blog/anxiety-files/201804/why-it-doesn-t-feel-good-when-someone-else-succeeds

Personal Needs: Meet Maslow: How Understanding the Priorities of Those Around Us Can Lead To Harmony And Improvement - Landon T. Smith, *CreateSpace Independent Publishing Platform,* April 26, 2017.

Tiger Woods: Tiger Woods - Jeff Benedict and Armen Keteyian, *Simon & Schuster*, April 2, 2019.

Chapter 9

Habits: How to Stop Procrastinating: A Simple Guide to Mastering Difficult Tasks - Steve Scott, *Oldtown Publishing LLC*, June 6, 2018.

Beliefs: Believe It to Achieve It: Overcome Your Doubts, Let Go of the Past, and Unlock Your Full Potential - Brian Tracy, *Tarcherperigee*, December 26, 2017.

Chapter 10

Memories: The Power of Your Subconscious Mind – Joseph Murphy, *Wilder Publications*, November 24, 2008.

Other Books By Shane K Twede

Nonfiction

Available in print and eBook at all online stores.
Personal development, business, and leadership:
Dress for Transformation

Fiction

Available in print and eBook at all online stores.
Action-Adventure:
TRINITY OPERATIONS series. Fast-paced military-style crime novels.
Escape From Ludomania
Ghost Assets

Childrens:
THE ADVENTURES OF DERBY & CHARLIE series; Key Life Lessons for children.
Derby and Charlie go to the Beach—Influence
Derby and Charlie go Fishing—Attitude

About Shane K. Twede

Shane K. Twede is an author, commercially-licensed pilot, and life coach. He is the creator of the Trinity Operations Novels and the popular children's book series The Adventures of Derby & Charlie.

Shane received his bachelor's degree in Professional Aeronautics from Embry Riddle University, an Associate of Arts degree from Big Bend CC in Washington State, and an Applied Science degree from South Seattle CC. He was born in the State of Washington and has spent much of his life working in the business world, from simple start-ups to Fortune 500 companies. Shane has worked for the following companies: Shell Global, Galvin Flying, The Boeing Company, Flight Tech, Harbor Airlines, *Seattle Times*, *Post Intelligencer*, Obrien Manor, Bellevue Athletic Club, Turkey House, and Barney Googles.

Shane is an adventure enthusiast, and enjoys camping, boating, flying, music, health and fitness, organic gardening, cooking, and life coaching.

Connect with Shane online:

https://shanektwede.com/

Parlar.com/shanetwede

Facebook.com/shanektwede

Acknowledgements

Thanks to my Lord and Savior, Jesus Christ. Through him all things are possible.

Thanks to all my mentors, those who took the time to speak up and teach me or lived a life worth emulating. Your investment lifted me on your shoulders so I could see further.

Thanks to Joy Martinez for your comprehensive editing—and snarky comments. Thanks to Kory Twede for the cover design and continual inspiration. And finally, thanks to my wife, Kathy Twede for your love and encouragement in all my endeavors.

www.ingramcontent.com/pod-product-compliance
Lightning Source LLC
Chambersburg PA
CBHW051430290426
44109CB00016B/1494